52nd STREET BE

Modern Jazz Drummers 1945-1965 by *Joe Hunt*

CONTENTS

Introduction

Many of us have witnessed a remarkable evolutionary phase of American popular music called jazz. The peak of its development—modern jazz—occurred between 1945 and 1965. My life as a drummer has been largely devoted to listening, studying, and playing jazz, and I'm grateful to have made a career in this wonderful music. My playing career began in 1954 in Richmond Indiana with the great alto saxophonist John Pierce, and continued in 1956 at Bloomington Indiana where I was fortunate to have been David Baker's drummer. My recording career began in NYC in 1960 with the George Russell sextet. I was his drummer until I was drafted into the Army in 1962. Stan Getz hired me for his quartet within a week after my separation in 1964, and I played with him for a year and a half. Early in 1966 Eddie Gomez and I joined Bill Evans's trio. I stayed for about a year into '67, then freelanced in NYC until the end of 1970. It was a privilege to have been close to some of the drummers about whom I have written, especially the Joneses (Elvin and "Philly Joe"). I heard them often, and sometimes they sat in on my jobs at *The Village Vanguard, Five Spot,* and *Birdland.*

In 1971 I moved from NY to Boston to join the faculty of Berklee College. In the fall of 1991 Berklee granted me a sabbatical leave to research this writing at Rutgers University with help from Dan Morgenstern and others at The Institute of Jazz Studies. I thank both the Institute and those at Berklee who supported the project, especially Tony Marvuglio for his advice and layouts. Thanks to them, and Jamey Aebersold's interest and suggestions, the book has been completed. I'm indebted to my wife, Ellen, whose patience, encouragement, and editing were indispensable.

I believe this is the first reference book of modern jazz drumming, although jazz scholars have made important contributions. Ira Gitler[1] and Leonard Feather[2] deserve credit for including information on the subject in their books and record liner notes. Dan Morgenstern's jazz wisdom has provided us with data of many jazz drummers, including liner information about Kenny Clarke.[3] Mike Hennessey is recognized for the first biography of a modern drumming master,[4] and Michael Haggerty for his complete discography.[5] The great Arthur Taylor has written a valuable book of interviews with other jazz musicians, some of whom are also master drummers.[6] Modern jazz drumming pedagogy is the subject of commendable books by drummers Alan Dawson,[7] Billy Mintz,[8] and Robert Kaufman.[9] Their books include both solo transcriptions and notated examples of phrases played (recorded) by important jazz drummers.

---

[1] *Jazz Masters of the Forties* Ira Gitler, 1983 DaCapo

[2] *The Book of Jazz* Leonard Feather, 1957 Horizon

[3] *Kenny Clarke* Swing LP 8411

[4] *Klook* Mike Hennessey, 1990 Quartet (London)

[5] *A Flower for Kenny* Michael Haggerty's discography/tribute for Kenny Clarke WHRB Boston 5/12/85

[6] *Notes and Tones* Arthur Taylor, 1977 DaCapo (new expanded edition)

[7] *A Manual For the Modern Drummer* Alan Dawson, 1964 Berklee Press

[8] *Different Drummers* Billy Mintz, 1984 Schirmer

[9] *The Art of Drumming* Robert Kaufman, 1993 Advance

There is currently more information about pre-modern jazz drumming than there is about drumming after 1945, although Burt Korall is now writing about modern jazz drummers to follow up *Drummin' Men*.[10] Gunther Schuller, who is preparing the third (modern jazz) book of his trilogy, has transcribed Chick Webb solos.[11] He has also brought new insights to the cymbal technique of Cuba Austin, the early swing drummer. An important text of early drumming, though not widely published, was written in 1976 by Theodore Dennis Brown[12] It is an extensive work in two volumes which includes both transcriptions and discographies of earlier jazz drummers, and is available from the University of Michigan library.

My book presents an abbreviated history of jazz to illustrate the progression of jazz drumming. Musical styles, which were responsible for the resulting drumming styles, are discussed. There is little emphasis on early jazz, swing, or fusion since none of these is the principal subject of the book. Merged into the history section is an account of the drum set's development. I have not included musical examples at this time, though I may write a follow-up in the future to include them.

Principal biographies follow. Kenny Clarke's innovations of the early forties were continued and developed by Max Roach and Roy Haynes later in the decade. In the fifties Art Blakey and "Philly Joe" Jones established a classic style. Following these men in the early sixties, Elvin Jones further liberated jazz drumming. His breakthroughs led to additional innovations by Anthony Williams. This synopsis of the developmental cycle is the basis of the seven principal biographies presented. Sid Catlett, Jo Jones, and Dave Tough are not included in this section, but their mini-bios are found in *Drummer Discography*. More information about them and their biographies is available in Burt Korall's *Drummin' Men*. Time lines and quotes are found in some of the principal biographies. Selected mini-discographies of all 216 drummers are listed alphabetically in the *Drummer Discography* section starting on page 51.

I've represented some of my fellow drummers in *Drummer Discography* by presenting each with an abbreviated selected discography—from one to four examples. In choosing the recordings I've balanced the factor of availability of those now on CD with out of print LPs. Small group, rather than big band recordings, are most often presented because the main source of the discography is *Modern Discography* by Bruyninckx, which includes few big band listings. Choice of recordings is mine, and not necessarily the artist's. An asterisk is placed in the left margin if I know the entry is outstanding. If no asterisk appears, it may be because I haven't heard the recording.

General criteria for entry are the following: activity from the period from 1945 to 1965 (a few drummers representing the late '60s and early '70s); drummers born before 1945 (1950) who contributed to the advancement of the modern jazz movement in America; drummers who have a substantial discography; swing drummers who participated in modernism as transition figures.

---

[10] *Drummin' Men* Burt Korall, 1989 Schirmer
[11] *The Swing Era* Gunther Schuller, 1989 Oxford Press, p. 298-9
[12] *A History and Analysis of Jazz Drumming to 1942* Theodore Dennis Brown, 1976 U. of Michigan

History, listing, and discography for the avant-garde period and its drummers is minimal. Percussionist and non-North American drummer inclusion is also minimal. There is no special reason for the final number of 216 entries. Initially I set a limit of 200, and then at the last minute asked the publisher for more pages. So an additional four pages (sixteen drummers) were added. Given time and space I could probably have gone on ad infinitum, but I stopped in order to accommodate layouts and page numbers. I offer my apologies to those drummers who are not included, and should have been.

Drummer Discography includes birth date. If no date is indicated, it is because I don't have the information. Recordings are dated by year if I don't know the day or month. *The New Grove Dictionary of Jazz* and Leonard Feather's *Encyclopedias of Jazz* are the references for the reference field. If a reference field is empty, it indicates that the drummer has not been represented in either of these sources. *Grove appears* in the reference field when the drummer is listed there. Inclusion in Leonard Feather's *Encyclopedias of Jazz* is indicated by Feather's name, followed by either *New* (which, coincidentally, is now old because it spans the 1940s to '50s) indicating *The New Encyclopedia of Jazz,* and/or '60s indicating *Jazz in the Sixties,* and/or '70s indicating *Jazz in the Seventies,* or *All* indicating inclusion in all three of Feather's works. Thank you Leonard Feather, and thanks to the *New Grove Dictionary of Jazz.*

The *Modern Drummer* magazine is another of my reference sources. *MD* has interviewed and/or written about many of the drummers listed, including all seven principal drummers. It is an excellent reference from which I have gathered much of my interview information. Thanks *MD,* and special thanks to Rick Mattingly for his permission to use parts of his interviews. Thanks to Theodore D. Brown, Gunther Schuller, Ira Gitler, Don DeMicheal, Chip Stern, Dan Riccio, Joseph Washek, Walter Pass, *Downbeat,* and all the other sources from which information has been gathered.

The movement toward modern jazz drumming began when drummers first shared active participation and comment within the ensemble dialogue. This concept is the very essence of African drumming, which was generally prohibited in North America when jazz began. The drum set was late finding its way into the music of jazz, and when it finally did it was often subdominant to the other instruments. This secondary role of drumming continued into modernism. Elvin Jones made a major contribution to the evolution of jazz by placing drumming back into its rightfully dominant role in the instrumental hierarchy during his partnership with John Coltrane in the early '60s. His drumming represents total liberation, following the 1940s innovations of pioneers Kenny Clarke and Max Roach. Early modernists had their foundation built by the great swing drummers. Style changed quickly, but tradition was modified gradually. Philly Joe Jones is a model of modernism where new concepts and tradition are balanced. Ed Blackwell represents the spirit of Warren Dodds while participating in experimental avant-garde dialogues. By the mid '60s jazz drummers were often recognized as leaders in the ensemble—liberated from traditional styles, yet inextricably connected to the tradition of their musical ancestors. My book is dedicated to all jazz musicians whose achievements set the pace for the art.

Early Jazz (1900-1930)

There is no traceable date for the beginning of jazz. Though there is evidence of jazz in the nineteenth century, the turn of the century is often used as a convenient reference mark. Since many of the first known jazz musicians came from New Orleans and played there, it is known as the birthplace of jazz and the place where "The New Orleans Style" developed. There has been valuable research about the origins of jazz in America. Of particular importance is Gunther Schuller's *Early Jazz* [13] and Theodore Dennis Brown's book of jazz drumming history. [14] The title of Brown's first chapter is "The African Influence on Jazz Drumming".

Jazz owes its origin to the Africans who were brought to America as slaves. They were often separated from their tribes during capture and marketing. Tribal integration and the Africans' natural ability to adapt to new situations were contributing factors to their assimilation into Western culture. Their drumming, a vital social expression, was/is a music of rhythmic sophistication, generally unfamiliar to the Western ear.

For this reason, some slave owners initiated a "prohibition of drumming". Drumming, however, continued to be practiced in other forms, since it was a primary source of communication among Africans and too much a part of their lives for them to give it up. As communication via the unique tribal languages of their music was curtailed, they found new outlets for their music in the church, and in minstrelsy, which embodied drumming via dance and body sounds. Minstrelsy, the precursor of Vaudeville, was entertainment by dancing, singing, and playing musical instruments such as tambourines, bones, barrels, or whatever else was available—as drum substitutes. It was popular in the nineteenth and early twentieth centuries and was performed by both African and European Americans. In "pattin' juba", the predecessor of tap dancing, the whole body became a drum. Another way that drums sneaked into minstrelsy was by the use of the banjo—which is, in fact, a drum with strings.

Congo Square was an area of New Orleans where, during the nineteenth century, slaves were permitted to dance and practice some of their tribal ceremonies. As the Congo Square activities were stopped (toward the turn of the century) musicians continued to play in orchestras and stage shows, but jazz was likely born in the parade (brass) bands of New Orleans. These legendary ensembles included trumpet (cornet), trombone, clarinet, and percussion. They played somber hymns as they marched—accompanying the casket of the deceased on the way to the funeral/burial—then broke into swinging high spirited jazz as they returned. Some of the first jazz improvisation began in brass bands, with the great trumpeters Buddy Bolden, King Oliver, and Louis Armstrong. Warren "Baby" Dodds (1898-1959), who was likely the first great jazz drummer, is said to have been a parade drumming specialist.

---

[13] *Early Jazz* Gunther Schuller, 1968 Oxford Press

[14] *A History and Analysis of Jazz Drumming to 1942* Theodore Dennis Brown, 1976 U of Michigan

Bass drum diameters sometimes reached as much as 30 inches, but widths were relatively shallow (10 to 14 inches). These measurements, with the exception of a slightly smaller diameter, did not change greatly until the 1940s and '50s. The bass drummer sometimes played both the cymbals (one hand held—the other mounted on the bass drum) and the bass drum at the same time. This was the first example of a drummer's playing that particular combination of instruments simultaneously. Since the 1920s they have both been pedaled. In 1910 a small metal pedal for the bass drum was manufactured by William F. Ludwig Sr. of Chicago. Its design was much like current models. Theodore Brown traces the actual invention of the first known foot pedal to Cornelius Ward, before 1840. With the invention of the bass drum pedal came the phenomenon of one player drumming on a set that was essentially just two drums—bass and snare. Later, a tiny Chinese tom-tom was added along with a small cymbal mounted flush to the batter head of the large marching size bass drum. These first drum sets were likely used in minstrel shows. Theodore Brown points out that the first snare drum stand was patented in 1898, indicating that before that time there was little, if any, reason for drummers to play in a sitting position.

Gut snares were used on the first military field/snare drums. They are similar to strings used by the violin family. Deep snare drums were used through the nineteenth century, but orchestral snare drums were used by some jazz drummers of New Orleans in the 1920s/1930s. There are early photos of Baby Dodds playing a shallow 5 inch snare drum. Much later, in the 1950s, very shallow (soprano) snare drums (3" to 4") were used by some modern jazz drummers. Around 1915 keys and thumb screws replaced ropes for tensioning the calf skin drum heads. By 1918 snare drums were built with a quick release device for the snare strainer.

Jazz appeared in dance halls of the Storyville district of New Orleans at about the same time that drummers were beginning to use the set. "Ragtime drummers" used traps (whistles, ratchets, bells, blocks, and sirens). They played in vaudeville shows and the first silent films. Jazz drummers Baby Dodds and Arthur "Zutty" Singleton (1898-1975) also used traps.

Ragtime drummer Tony Sbargo (1897-1969) played in an all white New Orleans band inappropriately named "The Original Dixieland Jazz Band". On their tours they excited largely white audiences. They were a hit in New York, and introduced the "jazz age" of the "roaring twenties" to the Northeast. The ODJB may have had an effect on the public similar to that of the Beatles in the '60s.

Between the end of World War I in 1918 and the great depression of the thirties, the US experienced a period of prosperity. New fashion, literature, and art had their musical counterpart in jazz, a music which expressed both gaiety and sadness. The improvisation of the jazz bands represented "taking a chance", which was the mood and climate of a young country ready for a change from conservatism. The prohibition movement (1920-1933) heightened the interest of many to seek illegitimate entertainment. Clubs called "speakeasies" provided drinks, jazz, and a party atmosphere. Jazz became popular as dance music, both here and in Europe.

Although various devices had been patented, it wasn't until 1920 that foot pedaled cymbals became part of the set. The first version of "foot cymbals", later to be called "sock cymbals", was named "the low boy", and preceded the "hi-hat" (circa 1928). The low boy was simply a lowered version of its successor; its cymbals were usually 10 inches in diameter and had deep cups, or bells. The higher instrument, which utilized a longer metal tube, was built by Walberg and Auge of Worcester Massachusetts.[15] Art Blakey credits drummer Kaiser Marshall with the invention of the hi-hat.[16]

The new raised height of the cymbals allowed drummers easier access to them with their hands (sticks). That it took eight years to raise the hi-hat up is a good clue to drumming styles of the '20s, which were centered around the snare drum.

Organists, pianists, and drummers found work in the theaters, playing for silent films until "talkies" were introduced in the late '20s. Drummers provided sound effects on "traps" as they coordinated with the visual action on the screen. Wire brushes, which first appeared as fly swatters, were used to duplicate railroad train sounds; jazz drummers used them for recording in the late '20s.

Since only a snare and bass drum were used at first, a technique known as "double drumming" was popular among early drummers. Sticks were used on the bass drum head as well as on the snare drum, thus providing a low sounding "tom-tom-like" function for the bass drum. Double drumming remained popular into the '40s.

The first tom-tom of the early '20s was a small, narrow Chinese drum (4x8 inches) with thick pigskin batter heads tacked onto its shell. It was clamped onto the bass drum hoop in a position similar to the left mounted small tom-tom of the '40s. During the twenties more equipment was added to the drum set. A woodblock and cowbell mounted to the bass were standard, and sets of bells and oriental temple blocks were often used. A Chinese cymbal of about 12 inches in diameter was likely the first suspended cymbal used in jazz bands. Its exotic sound was different from the orchestral cymbals. Small "choke" cymbals of 6 to 10 inches were later used for solo fills in the dance bands of the late '20s and early '30s.

Even though their equipment was primitive by today's standards, the first drum set players were extremely inventive and imaginative. Their snare drum technique and trap equipment developed as a direct result of their needs for special sounds related to their work in theaters, shows, and dance halls.

---

[15] Norm Scott provided this information

[16] *Modern Drummer* (9/84) p.11

The Swing Era (1930-1945)

The "roaring twenties" ended with the U.S. stock market crash of 1929 known as "Black Thursday" (10/24/29). This national disaster swiftly set the country into an economic depression that lasted well into the next decade. The 1930s were not prosperous times for musicians or most others in America. Franklin D. Roosevelt won the presidential election of 1932 (and was later re-elected in '36 and '40). His social reforms and industrial reconstruction policies supported a return to national vitality in the forties. War, which ended in 1945, also helped national economy.

Musical employment became more competitive because of the depression. By 1930 film sound tracks replaced live musicians in the theater. Ensemble size had been growing during the '20s, and by late in the decade big bands became a popular size ensemble for dance music.

Jazz music became regional in the 1930s. Chicago style, made famous by a group of mainly white players, remained close to its New Orleans roots of small ensembles. Warren "Baby" Dodds was teacher to three important Chicago drummers: George Wettling, Dave Tough, and Gene Krupa. Vic Berton was another important drummer from Chicago. Although he did not have the jazz reputation of the others, Berton's use of percussion instruments, including timpani, was innovative. During the 1930s New York was becoming the jazz center of the nation, and by 1950 most of the best players from Chicago and other major cities had moved there. As more of the 1930's bands made New York their headquarters, the city's recording business grew. Kansas City became known for its special brand of swing. Its blues-based style may have been the most authentic link to modernism. Hometown jazz bands in St. Louis, Cleveland, and other mid-western cities are also represented on recordings made in the '30s.

Drumming advanced mainly because of personal style and flexibility of the great drummers of the swing era. Major musical innovations were usually made by other instrumentalists. This is not to say that swing drummers were never innovative or that they weren't doing the right thing musically by deferring to the stylistic lead of the others. On the contrary, the invention of early jazz drumming techniques generally followed a sound and logical, if not exciting, musical direction. In some ways early drummers functioned similarly to the percussionists of European orchestras by adding extra touches to the already finished music. Percussion instrument technique was a prerequisite for most work. It's easy to understand this if we imagine the drum sets of the great swing drummers—Chick Webb's temple blocks—Sonny Greer's timpani and orchestral chimes.

Chick Webb's brilliant drum set solos inspired all the drummers of the '30s. Webb, who died in 1939 at the age of 37, was the first jazz drummer to successfully lead a big band. This was additional inspiration for his admirers Gene Krupa and Buddy Rich, who later also were band leaders. They became drum set super stars who played exciting extended solos and popularized "dance drumming" of the thirties and early forties. But their personal stardom and celebrity status did not dramatically influence the development of jazz drumming.

Krupa and Rich set a standard of excellence for drum technique and showmanship, but they did not provide conceptually innovative musical breakthroughs for others to follow. Drummers still played static quarter or half note beats, held in tempo with the rest of the rhythm section, to encourage and stimulate dancing. This time-keeping role continued for both drummer and bassist well into the '40s.

Hotel ballrooms and dance halls sponsored live radio broadcasts of big bands, which were heard throughout the country. Despite the depression, or maybe because of it, dancing to swing music was very popular in the 1930s. Swing arrangements played by big bands inspired lively dance steps such as the "jitterbug".

Dance marathons and contests created work for musicians. Occasionally, rival bands were challenged at "cutting contests", where two bands were hired to play opposite each other. Some bands gained national popularity comparable to that of athletic teams. Many still hold legendary status. Arrangements, which by now were an important component of the music, called for reading and/or keen listening skills from drummers.

Benny Goodman introduced racially mixed groups in concerts at Carnegie Hall in 1937 and '38. There, members of Count Basie's band joined Goodman's players in jam sessions, marking one of the first times that jazz bands were publicly integrated.

New tom-tom designs were the most significant changes for drum sets of the '30s. A floor tom-tom with a tunable top head was available in 1931. In 1937 the Leedy Drum Co. introduced tom-toms with separate tension for both top and bottom heads, and by the end of the '30s the standard was almost complete for the basic drum set essentially as it remains today.

The "golden age" of America's popular music began in the 1930s and continued into the '40s. We still draw from the tunes written then. Bands and vocalists were recording songs by Gershwin, Porter, and other American composers. From today's perspective, jazz was not at its cutting edge during the swing era, but it was high quality popular music. Dancing audiences popularized swing—the swing era was an exciting time, but as the '40s approached there was little advancement of innovative improvisation within the big bands.

One exception was Lester Young, the first modern saxophonist, and another was Jonathan "Papa Jo" Jones, the legendary swing drummer. Both played with the famous Count Basie band from Kansas City. Jo Jones's loose style and innovative hi-hat technique were critical influences to modern jazz drumming styles later in the '40s.

Swing to Bop/Early Modernism (1940-1950)

At the start of the decade and through the mid forties, the "swing era" entered a transition toward modernism. The dance bands of the late '30s remained popular into the forties, and early modernists found work in them. They became vehicles for the first modern arrangers and for the first recorded modern jazz solos. Due to a recording ban by the American Federation of Musicians from 1942 to 1943/5, recorded jazz history from that period is limited. Nevertheless, the records made preceding the ban, and recordings of radio shows (called "air checks") made during the ban, provide us with an accounting. In addition, copies of recordings of previously exclusive special military service variety shows featuring music of that period have been made available recently. These are called "V discs"—V for victory—the hope of America, then at war.

Americans continued to enjoy dancing to swing music. But beyond this interest in dancing, there may have been a kind of artistic tension which slowly gained momentum during the recording ban and found release by the end of the war in 1945. Some of this was a natural evolution of the music on its own terms, as it was striving for its place apart from the boundaries of dance music.

We are indebted to the early drummers whose contributions were the genesis of modern drumming. However, it seems to me that creative freedom in jazz drumming was first realized when Kenny Clarke and Max Roach began to establish musical dialogue in the bands they played with in the '40s. Clarke was to drumming what Lester Young was to saxophone or clarinet playing. It is difficult to categorize Young as a modernist, because of his roots in swing. Yet his influence upon younger modern players like Stan Getz and Hank Mobley is so profound that he must be included with them. Clarke is much the same.

Like his contemporary Sid Catlett, and predecessor Chick Webb, Clarke's style was strongly personal. His knowledge of trombone, xylophone, and composition provided him with a unique perspective of the drummer's interaction with soloists and ensemble. Clarke's concept was profound, yet quite simple—the drummer should be included as an equal partner in the democracy of the band.

His use of broken time—breaking the constant bass drum pulse—in the early '40s, was the first step toward modern jazz drumming styles. His approach was basic, yet subtly revolutionary. Clarke noticed that when he left out constant quarter notes on his bass drum at very fast tempo, the feeling of the rhythm loosened up. This also liberated the bass drum so it could be used more effectively to support, or fill in between, ensemble figures. This technique, ominously called "bomb dropping", turned out to be the beginning of modern drumming.

It's hard to imagine such a judicious and musical drummer being fired for his drum phrasing (Teddy Hill's band circa 1940). But at that time jazz styles in general, and drumming styles in particular, were late in their development.

During a discussion of that period Clarke recalls, "Frank (bassist, brother) had bought a record of a Duke Ellington session featuring Jimmy Blanton and we listened to it over and over and agreed that drumming had to change to accommodate the new bass style."[17] So, for all his brilliance, Kenny Clarke's playing represented a long overdue liberation of musical logic as much as an innovative drumming style.

Klook's participation in the famous 1941 Harlem jam sessions allowed him to experiment freely with his new ideas. His colleagues at *Minton's* included other innovators—Charlie Christian, Dizzy Gillespie, and Thelonious Monk. These men were the founding fathers of the first modern jazz, called bebop. Max Roach says, "Dizzy, for me, was actually the catalyst of that whole bebop period. Bebop restructured the harmonic notions of the music, and it changed the rhythms."[18]

Although modernism (bop) was known as revolutionary music, it evolved from, and was directly linked with, its swing ancestry during this important transitional partnership. A few of the other swing drummers also experimented with techniques we now take for granted; for example, riding the cymbal instead of, or in addition to, using the bass drum to keep time. But conservatism in drumming generally prevailed.

Drummers of the early '40s continued to find work in big dance bands. Consequently, their equipment remained generally unchanged until later in the decade when jazz became popular in NYC jazz cabarets, where smaller drums were preferred. There were other reasons for smaller, more muffled bass drums.

The ride cymbal was beginning to take on a new role in its relationship to the bass player's notes. Previously, the bass drum had been used to support and lengthen the bass player's staccato notes, but as bassists began to "walk" in a more modern style, their notes became more legato. The ride cymbal began to replace some of the bass drum's function of sustaining sound, as it complimented the bass violin in a new way. This was the manifestation of Kenny Clarke's original vision.

As bebop drums of the late '40s-'50s became smaller, cymbals grew larger. Bass drums of 22 and 24 inch diameters replaced the larger drums of the '30s, and by 1950, 20 inch bass drums were used. Larger cymbal sizes became popular for both the hi-hat (14-15 inch diameters) and the new ride cymbal (16-24 inch diameters).

The larger size, in combination with the increased weight and thickness of the ride cymbal, allowed for a clear stick attack within its drone of sound resulting from repeated hits. The cymbal's legato, ringing sound was used for textural ostinati as well as for rhythmic accents, and thus a new background color enhanced the music. Dave Tough is known for his unusual and exotic ride cymbal sound with the Woody Herman band. It may have been a Turkish K. Zildjian because of its dark, low tone.

[17] Kenny Clarke interview, Helen Oakley Dance (Rutgers jazz archives)

[18] Max Roach interview, Gene Santoro *Pulse* magazine12/88

The earliest bop prototype can be found in the recordings of Charlie Parker, a young saxophonist from Kansas City who was nicknamed "Yardbird", and later "Yard" or "Bird". His first recordings available to the public were made on 4/30/41 with Jay McShann's band for *Decca*.[19] Even though Parker's solos were brief, they formed complete mini-compositions which instantly outlined the essence of modern jazz. He was certainly influenced by his predecessors and drew from their strengths, but his playing included a new sophisticated polyrhythmic vocabulary which set him apart from others. His leadership of the new bop movement is unquestionable, and his influence is awesome.

Shadow Wilson,[20] at age twenty-three, may have been the first modern drummer to record with Bird in 1942, followed by Max Roach in 1945. Otherwise, Bird's earliest recording accompanists (1940-45) were usually drummers known for their great swing. These include Gus Johnson who played with him in Jay McShann's band, Sid Catlett, Specs Powell, Harold West, Cozy Cole, and J.C. Heard. Even the New Orleans pioneer Zutty Singleton (1898-1975) recorded with him in 1945.[21] These men, and other popular 1940's swing drummers including Jo Jones, Dave Tough, and Buddy Rich played a special role in the development of early modern jazz.

They deserve credit not only for raising the level of swing drumming to a standard of excellence for all time, but for their flexibility in providing fine accompaniment to the early modernists. They were effective not because of their innovative drumming, but for their confident and conservative time playing which allowed the other players maximum rhythmic freedom for melodic experiments. In the early '40s these drummers were vital transitional figures who helped bridge swing to modern jazz. They were consummate accompanists.

Buddy Rich, an important figure in big band swing drumming of the '30s and '40s, made an interesting recording in 1950 with a modern group featuring Charlie Parker, Dizzy Gillespie, Curly Russell, and Thelonious Monk.[22] Though not a modernist himself, Rich's unequaled drumming technique allowed him active participation with them. In the '50s Rich led his own bop-influenced band, and in the '60s and '70s his big bands played "jazz rock" repertoire. His example is unique, but it represents the high level of consistency and flexibility that swing drumming had reached by the 1940s. This is one of the reasons it was not so easy for drummers of the early '40s to change their style to a truly modern approach.

---

[19] First issued on single Decca 78s (4/30/41), later Decca LP DL9236, currently CD reissue *Blues From K.C.* Jay McShann Decca GRP GRD-614

[20] Listed as the possible drummer on a 1942 Chicago broadcast recording. To date, the session is not available: Charlie Parker discography by Akira Yamamato 8/83 included with the 10 record box collection; *The Complete Charlie Parker On Verve* (Japan) 00MJ 3268/77

[21] *The Genius of Charlie Parker* Charlie Parker (2/28/45) Savoy CD SV-0130

[22] *Bird and Diz, The Genius of Charlie Parker #4* Charlie Parker (6/6/50)Verve CD 831 133-2; tracks also in LP box Verve (Japan) 00MJ 3268/77; and US CD box *Bird* Verve 83714254, with extra tracks

A few, however, began to follow Clarke's lead toward musical liberation. Most, including Clarke himself, were not virtuosic soloists like Webb and Rich. They were more concerned with ensemble participation. Nevertheless Clarke, in his special way, was an innovative soloist. His buoyant use of rudimental rolls and grace notes give his phrasing melodic (linear) character.

Sid Catlett introduced three part linear phrasing between snare drum (with brushes), bass drum, and crash cymbal, in his four bar solo trades with bassist Slam Stewart on Lester Young's quartet recording of "I Never Knew".[23] Though new ideas like his were proved, the solos of early modern drummers still seemed to rely as much on tradition as on exploration of original concepts. Conservatism generally remained the choice of most drummers until the mid '40s, when Max Roach introduced a more completed version of Catlett's and Clarke's earlier work.

By 1945 a growing number of serious modernists had set up a national network through which they shared concepts and played the new music, bop. Unwittingly, these players had formed an exclusive community which required proficiency in a new jazz language. This included knowledge of altered scales, harmonic tensions, polyrhythms, polymetric phrasing, and the ability to play at fast tempo. However, instead of following these academic criteria, they more than likely just studied Bird's latest records.

Several jazz cabarets opened on 52nd St., NYC, which became the famous "Street"—bop center of the forties. Dizzy Gillespie and Charlie Parker, who were regulars there, were joined by an emerging group of precocious young modern players including Bud Powell, Al Haig, Miles Davis, and the innovative Max Roach.

The 1945 Charlie Parker recordings for *Savoy* are excellent examples of Roach's important step—the second one, after Clarke's—toward jazz drumming's liberation. His new drumming concepts made use of the set as a complete ensemble instrument on its own terms—as a choir—with alto, tenor, bass, etc. On his earliest Parker and Powell records he uses the cymbals as a drum substitute, in place of tom-toms, used later. This integration of sounds fostered dialogues between the instruments of the set which, in turn, provided new input to ensemble participation.

Creative freedom in jazz drumming was further developed by Max Roach as he experimented with his new musical conversations in the bop bands of the mid '40s. There were two separate but interrelated components of his success:

1. The continuation of Clarke's idea—bringing and sustaining a musical logic to the ensemble—a more participatory role for the drummer

2. The assertion of his own self confident musical voice within the ensemble

---

[23] *The Complete Lester Young* Lester Young (12/28/43) Mercury (Japan) CD 830 920-2

His important new step was similar to that of Jimmy Blanton's liberation of the bass violin in the late '30s. Like Blanton, Max Roach compels his listener to pay attention as he quickly achieves instrumental equality. As Blanton (in the '40s) bowed, Roach (in 1958) used timpani, and recorded with a percussion ensemble.[24] His concepts initiated new interest and a welcome alternative to traditionalism.

Roy Haynes was another early modernist who brought to fruition a more fully developed realization of Clarke's innovations. He replaced Max Roach in the 1949 bands of Bird, Miles, and Bud Powell. Even though he followed Roach, Haynes quickly established his own special voice within these outstanding groups. It is common to see either one of them as the drummer on most of the great bop records of the late '40s and early '50s.

Jazz compositions of the late '40s called for new interpretative skills from drummers. Straight time on the cymbals remained a popular accompaniment, but compositions by Bird, Dizzy, and Monk were often intricate and syncopated. Gillespie, who had encouraged Kenny Clarke to experiment earlier, expected his drummers to meet the challenge of arrangements like "Things to Come". Classic bop lines "Shaw 'Nuff", "Ko Ko", "Donna Lee", "Constellation", "Cheryl", "Crazeology" ("Bud's Bubble") and "Royal Roost" ("Tenor Madness") illustrate the exciting new phrasing.

Denzil Best, in addition to being a master of the wire brushes, was also a trumpet player and popular bebop composer. His compositions include "Move",[25] "Wee",[26] and "Dee Dee's Dance".[27]

Since 78 rpm records permitted a maximum of about three minutes playing time, solos were abbreviated. Nevertheless, in these late '40s recordings we begin to hear drummers included in the soloing—occasionally playing an introduction and/or briefly exchanging four bar solos with other band members before the last chorus. A solo technique of choice is often a "walking cymbal" ostinato with figures played independently between snare and bass drums. Max Roach uses this solo technique on several of his early recordings with Parker on *Dial* and *Savoy*.

Roach applied independence (p.15) with a new twist on Sonny Stitt's 1949 recording of "Sonny Side".[28] After Bud Powell's piano solo there is a wonderful sixteen bar drum solo/duet between him and Roach just before a bass solo. After their first eight bars, Roach begins to break the second eight bars into solo phrases of two bar groups—the first two bars without cymbal time and the second two with it. This segues nicely into the bridge of Curly Russell's walking bass solo, which completes the chorus before the last head. The entire take is two minutes and twenty one seconds long, timed just right for a ten inch 78 single record, which is how it was originally released in the early fifties.

---

[24] *Max Roach with the Boston Percussion Ensemble* Max Roach (8/17/58) Mercury Stereo LP 80015

[25] *The Birth of the Cool* Miles Davis (1/21/49) Blue Note CD B221Y-92862

[26] aka "Allen's Alley" *The Bebop Revolution* 52nd Street All Stars (2/27/46) RCA Bluebird 2177-2- RB

[27] *Be Bop Revisited* Chubby Jackson (1/20/48) Xanadu (France) EPM CD FDC 5174

[28] *Sonny Stitt/Bud Powell/J.J. Johnson* Sonny Stitt (12/11/49) Prestige OJCCD-009-2

Afro-Cuban jazz played by Charlie Parker with Machito's orchestra led to interest in mixing jazz and Latin styles. Latin rim beats on the snare drum (snares off) was another favorite solo technique. These beats were variations of rhumba and other authentic South American music originally played on timbales and congas. Roy Haynes uses this Latin technique in the last eight bar drum solo bridge of the out head on a 1949 Bud Powell recording of "52nd Street Theme".[29] The first six bars of Latin beats are contrasted with four strong downbeats (half notes) on the bass drum in the last two bars of the bridge.

The four bass drum notes represent a kind of "signal" which ends the solo and sets up the band's entrance. Signals like this became commonly used by drummers as their solos concluded. Later, in the '50s, Art Blakey was known for his famous two and four bar cadential signals after longer solos—and still later, in the '60s, Tony Williams used a Miles Davis cliché as his concluding signal trademark (Dit-di-dit-di-dit).

Small ensemble interaction, although limited by today's standards, was a characteristic of modern jazz drumming of the '40s. Drummers and pianists began to form accompaniment patterns together. The fast tempos of bebop called for new facility for drummers' hands and feet. The bass drum was used to play accents as well as to keep time, although the time keeping function continued into the '60s. Odd meters were almost never used in jazz until the '50s. Except for Afro-Cuban 6/8, the meter of '40s bebop was exclusively 4/4.

Examples of the new freedom in modern drumming are found in all the recordings of Charlie Parker. Some of his more modern accompanists of the late '40s include Max Roach, Kenny Clarke, Roy Haynes, Don Lamond, Roy Porter, Shelly Manne, and Joe Harris (Art Blakey and Ed Shaughnessy in 1950). These recordings tell us a great deal about changing drumming styles from 1945 to 1950.

Over the next fifteen years the concept of independent coordination for drummers became important. This idea was presented in the late '40s by jazz drummer and renown educator Jim Chapin, in one of the first books to deal with the subject.[30] Chapin formulated a system of exercises where the right hand and left foot play a continuous ostinato on a ride cymbal and hi-hat respectively, while the left hand and right foot perform integrated phrases between the snare and bass drums. His classic text also includes written (rhythm) melodies for the drummer to play. The etudes are linked to techniques used by Max Roach, Roy Haynes, and Art Blakey. Chapin credits Art Blakey as the first drummer of the late '40s to use a dominant foot ostinato with the hi-hat on beats two and four.

---

[29] *The Amazing Bud Powell* volume1 Bud Powell (5/1/51) Blue Note CD B21Y-81503

[30] *Advanced Techniques for the Modern Drummer* Jim Chapin,1948 (published by author) RR #2 Box 1017 Elizabeth Street, Sag Harbor, NY 11963

Development of Modernism (1950-1960)

Jazz record sales moved well enough by 1950 to create a small demand for artists to record more new music. They made a sizable inventory of quality recordings (many of which are now available as reissues). *Blue Note* record series titles *New Sounds In Modern Music* and *New Faces, New Sounds,* reflect the climate of experimentation. Originality was encouraged and promoted by small independent record companies, with high quality performance taken for granted. Jazz of the '50s often symbolized non-music movements—nonconformity and existentialism, then fashionable.

Creative musical momentum was in place. Nevertheless, splinter musical groups did not always support each other's interests. The "east coast" vs. "west coast" jazz controversy of the mid '50s tended to stereotype and polarize both "schools" of jazz. Each had merit and represented healthy artistic diversity. Led on by jazz writers and critics, many fans began to favor one style over the other. Ironically, the favoritism which began as a result of the movement's diversity eventually hindered its momentum.

An important recording which has been rare until recently is the classic Miles Davis nonet's (nine member ensemble) *The Birth Of The Cool.*[31] These *Capitol* recording sessions in 1949-50 represent a major achievement in small ensemble composition and orchestration. The arrangements—collaborations of Miles Davis, Gil Evans, and Gerry Mulligan—include French horn and tuba as well as trumpet, trombone, alto and baritone saxophones. The rhythm section's interaction with ensemble figures and solos is exemplary. Because there were three different recording sessions (each with a different rhythm section), we have an opportunity to compare interpretations by Kenny Clarke and Max Roach within the same band.

Two fine recordings which helped introduce "west coast" jazz were subsequently made in Los Angeles. These were by Shorty Rogers, who used similar horn/tuba instrumentation for his octet in 1951,[32] and Gerry Mulligan, a writer for *The Birth Of The Cool,* who in 1953 recorded his own tentet album.[33] Shelly Manne appeared on the Rogers session, while Chico Hamilton and Larry Bunker shared the drumming for the Mulligan tentet.

As the title of the Miles album indicates, all three of these outstanding recordings are examples of so-called "cool" jazz. A healthy, productive musical climate for individuality and quality existed during this period and, thanks to the high standards set by the previously mentioned artists, there were few poor jazz recordings made. Surviving catalogs of both the major and smaller independent jazz record companies confirm this.

---

[31] Originally 78 singles, then Capitol 10" LP, later 12" LP *The Birth of the Cool* Miles Davis, currently CD reissue *The Birth of the Cool* Blue Note B21Y-92862

[32] *Modern Sounds* Shorty Rogers, first 45s, then Capitol 10" LP, later 12" LP collection, currently CD reissue *The Birth of the Cool volume 2* Blue Note B21Y-98935

[33] *Tentet* Gerry Mulligan, first 45s, then Capitol 10" LP, later 12" LP collection, currently CD reissue *The Birth of the Cool volume 2* Blue Note B21Y-98935

During the bebop era, heroin use was not uncommon. Bird, the movement's leader, was an addict, though he publicly warned against drug use—claiming that it was not musically beneficial. His private life of excess, well known and imitated by many of his followers, resulted in his death in 1955 at age 34. Similarly, other young jazz musicians also lost their lives. It is unfortunate that there were no addiction treatment programs as we have now, and that there was little information about addictive drugs, including alcohol.

Even though the private lives of some modernists were eccentric and occasionally even tragic, they must be given credit for outstanding musical achievements. Many of these artistic revelations remain incomparable. The great Rossiere "Shadow" Wilson died at age forty in 1959. His discography reveals that he backed many important bands, with a special blend of modern swing. In 1957 he recorded with Thelonious Monk and John Coltrane.[34]

Jazz drummer/arranger, Norman "Tiny" Kahn died in 1953 at the age of 29. Tiny's big band arrangements such as "Godchild"[35] remain classics of modern jazz of the late '40s and early '50s. His musical influence, like Shadow Wilson's on drummers of the fifties, was subtle, but crucial. Mel Lewis credits Kahn, who was a favorite sideman of Stan Getz, with shaping his ensemble concepts. Other Getz drummers of the '50s include Wilson, Roy Haynes, Stan Levey, Don Lamond, Walter Bolden, Al Levitt, and Detroiters Art Mardigan and Frank Isola.

An interesting drum fill cliché which had been evolving since the mid '40s is the "surprise" fill. This, like the early bombs, is one or more accents seemingly from "out of nowhere" which catches the listener's attention. Don Lamond uses several of these on Woody Herman's record title *Keeper Of the Flame*, originally released as a single 78 in 1950 (and now reissued as a CD).[36] Roy Haynes sometimes uses sixteenth note anticipations, as on the blues "Back in the Cage"[37]—one snare drum accent just before the down beat of bar seven of the first trumpet solo chorus (following the piano solo).

Another cliché is the four or eight bar drum solo made deliberately complex—the drummer plays out of time or "off center" and then comes back on the down beat. Shelly Manne plays such solo fills on the final shout chorus of "More Moon",[38] which is also on the Woody Herman CD *Keeper of the Flame*.

It is said that pianist/teacher Lennie Tristano did not care much for most drummers in general, and particularly not for their surprises. He was a strict disciplinarian to many of his drummers, and had them play only time, with minimum fills and solos for whole tunes. They had to learn his intricate compositions to be able to support the accents of the melodic lines. Harold Granowsky, Denzil Best, Al Levitt, Jeff Morton, Shelly Manne, and Arthur Taylor were some of the drummers who accompanied him on recordings.

---

[34] *Thelonious Monk and John Coltrane* Thelonious Monk (7/1/57) Jazzland OJCCD-039

[35] *The Bebop Era* (2/24/49) Columbia CD CK 40972

[36] *Keeper of the Flame* Woody Herman (12/20/49) Capitol CDP 7 98453 2

[37] *Portrait of Art Farmer* Art Farmer (5/1/58) Contemporary OJCCD-166-2

[38] *Keeper of the Flame* Woody Herman (7/20/49) Capitol CDP 7 98453 2

The trend to use smaller drums, which had begun in the late '40s, continued into the 1950s. Soprano and alto snare drums were endorsed by Roy Haynes for the Ludwig Company in the mid '50s. They were 3x13 or 4x14 inches. By 1955 the 14x20 inch bass drum was almost as popular as the 14x22, and by the end of the decade 14x18 inch bass drums were available. The 14x14 inch floor tom-tom became an alternative to the 16x16. The same is true of the 8x12 inch mounted tom-tom for the 9x13.

Early in the 1950s a small mounted bongo drum was used by Chico Hamilton, who was also one of the first to use a very small bass drum. Modern jazz drummers generally did not use small percussion instruments, although occasionally a cowbell is heard on tunes from 1950's records like Bud Powell's "Un Poco Loco" (see page 31) and Art Blakey's live *Birdland* version of "A Night in Tunisia".[39]

Blakey was one of the first to use a sizzle ride cymbal. Many metal rivets were installed around his cymbal's outer edge for the effect. An invention of the '50s was the cymbal tilter, a small device which screwed onto the top of the cymbal holder rod and tilted the cymbal toward the player. This raised the height of the cymbals, still keeping them within reach, and gave a new look to the drum sets of the late '50s. Drum companies have since included the design as a standard feature for all their cymbal stands. There were new pedal designs and other hardware improvement during the '50s.

But the most important innovation of the 1950s was surely the plastic drum head introduced by Remo Beli. Synthetic drum heads offer the following benefits:

1. Drummers no longer have to "tuck" or prepare their drum heads on hoops for use. Tucking, the only alternative to purchasing pre-mounted heads at substantially higher prices, is somewhat difficult and time consuming

2. Much less tensioning is necessary when weather conditions change and affect the drum head's pitch and tension. (Beli's company, *Remo*, appropriately named their new heads *Weather King*)

3. They are not as easily punctured

Drummers of the late '50s were quick to make the change to synthetic drum heads, and by the 1960s there were few drummers who used calf skin heads on any of their drums. But the compromise in sound quality did not appeal to some. Mel Lewis never did give up using calf heads, at least not on his drums' batter sides.

Mel's solution was also used by Jimmy Cobb and some of the other jazz drummers of the late '50s and early '60s. For their snare drum set up they kept a calf batter head on the top and a synthetic snare head on the underside. This allowed them to continue playing their brushes on the more familiar texture of the calf skin drum head. Later, in the '80s, a variety of head types were developed, including a textured snare drum batter head for use with brushes.

---

[39] *A Night at Birdland* volume1 Art Blakey (2/21/54) Blue Note CD B21Y-46519

By the mid '50s several important bop musicians had literally burned out and died due to excesses of life's temptations. This must have been confusing for their followers, who then were required to look elsewhere for creative signals toward the future. The intensity of the early bebop of the middle and late '40s gradually gave way to relaxed alternatives in the mid '50s. Some of the new styles, which themselves began as experiments, were called "cool" and "progressive" jazz. The modern-classical influence (progressive jazz) was popularized in the mid '50s by Stan Kenton's band.

Shelly Manne moved from New York to California in 1952 to become a leader of "west coast" jazz there. Stan Levey and Mel Lewis, also native New Yorkers, made LA their home as well. Levey, who had been to Hollywood earlier in 1946 with Dizzy Gillespie's *Tempo Jazzmen* to record for *Dial* records, settled there in 1952. Lewis was the only one of the three who returned to NYC to stay in 1962. All three played, in the order listed, with Stan Kenton's big band. Native Californians Chico Hamilton and Larry Bunker, mentioned earlier, were popular LA recording artists of the 1950s. Lawrence Marable and Frank Butler both represent the so-called "California hard" bop style. Their fine work influenced a younger precocious Californian, Billy Higgins.

On the east coast (NYC), recordings of new drummers—Arthur Taylor, Lex Humphries, Philly Joe Jones, Specs Wright, Charlie Persip, Louis Hayes, Jimmy Cobb and others, along with the continuing work of Art Blakey, Roy Haynes, Max Roach, Kenny Clarke, and Shadow Wilson—demonstrate classic modern jazz drumming styles of the fifties.

Arthur Taylor was, and remains, a vital and very influential NYC drummer who, like Roach and Haynes, worked extensively with Charlie Parker, Bud Powell, and Miles Davis. His vast discography is consistently excellent. I had the good fortune to hear him play with the *Charlie Parker with Strings* group at *Birdland* in 1953. His drumming is simultaneously graceful and powerful. When I saw him in NYC in 1990, I was reminded of the virtuosity of his solo drumming, reminiscent of Buddy Rich.

By 1955 there had been considerable development within the diverse styles of modernism. Significant musical achievements were realized though public interest in some styles began to diminish. In 1953,'54, and '55, *The Modern Jazz Quartet* (MJQ) recorded albums which represented successful fusion of jazz with traditional classical music. The original group included vibist Milt Jackson, bassists Ray Brown or Percy Heath, and pianist John Lewis whose vision and leadership is responsible for the group's origin and longevity. Kenny Clarke, pioneer of modern drumming, was the group's original drummer.[40]

The great Connie Kay became the quartet's drummer in 1955 [41] and remains with them as of this writing. The MJQ's jazz authenticity became the subject of minor controversy in the late '50s. This is regrettable not only because it should never have been questioned in the first place, but also because their distinctive accomplishments deserved endorsement and support instead of criticism.

---

[40] *MJQ*   MJQ (12/22/52) Prestige OJCCD-125-2,
   Django   MJQ (6/25/53) Prestige OJCCD-057-2
[41] *Concorde* MJQ (7/2/55)   Prestige OJCCD-002-2

John Coltrane came up in bands that played "rhythm and blues", the popular African American music of the 1950s. At the same time, jazz played by predominantly white players became popular with largely white audiences. Some of these bands were interesting, but the contrived use of European classicism and neoclassicism by some did not especially contribute to substantive jazz improvisation.

These issues raise the question of authenticity as related to the African American ancestry of jazz, and may account for at least part of the increase of racial polarization of players by the late '50s and early '60s. The earlier bebop code called for high level musicianship regardless of color. Even if racism existed, it would generally be subjugated by the player's ability to communicate clearly on his/her instrument.

As modern jazz diversified, the original language that had been spelled out by Bird was no longer the universal reference for all players. In the mid '50s new dialects, if not languages, were taking shape to accommodate new musical ideas. Consequently, performance criteria became less uniform. The following were two points of view:

1. New playing styles called for new performance criteria, whether or not these styles were directly related to preceding jazz styles

2. New performance criteria were unnecessary and premature since much of the music in question was not valid jazz in the first place, either by authentic African American standards or by the high level of musical standards universally accepted earlier

Some of the new individual styles in question promoted more new (baby) styles which became slightly off balance and less responsible to their predecessors (parents). Jazz, then, may have taken a premature step in its evolution.

Diversity—a source of development and interest earlier—no longer supported a unified movement. The next generation of younger players (not the established jazz greats) were most affected. We see this clearly now, as there has been no comparable significant advancement or leadership in jazz since the 1960s.

Due in part to drug related problems, a negative public image of bop had developed and national support waned. Between the mid and late '50s America had lost much of its enthusiasm for jazz, in general, and bop, in particular. One could consider this period as the end of bop as a popular music—whatever small popularity it still held—with no comparable authentic jazz style to replace it.

Interestingly, there was then a minor revival of traditional "mainstream" jazz which offered a more basic alternative. Bop seemed to be going the way of its swing predecessor—retired and acknowledged as an important veteran, though without honor. But time would soon tell that its development was far from over.

In the late '50s bop went underground to the African American communities of larger US cities and to Europe, where it was still appreciated. By 1960 several prominent American jazz musicians including Bud Powell, Stan Getz, and Kenny Clarke had moved to Europe. Predominantly African American groups, such as Art Blakey's *Jazz Messengers,* continued to perform in the tradition of Bird. Their music, sometimes called "hard bop", achieved both relaxation and strong statement of purpose.

There are classic jazz recordings made by at least five different groups of *Jazz Messengers* led by Blakey from 1954 to 1964.[42] Early movement toward racial liberation was directly associated with this phase of jazz, which was in the process of reclaiming its authentic roots and simplifying its language. The term "free jazz" is appropriate to describe the developments of the early '60s—with previews in the late '50s by John Coltrane, George Russell, Charles Mingus, and Ornette Coleman.

The career of Miles Davis is an excellent reference for a concise overview of the entire modern period from 1945. In that year, Bird made his first recording under his own name for *Savoy* records.[43] At the now famous session Miles made his first major recording debut. In 1950 he completed the *Birth Of The Cool* session mentioned earlier. In 1955 he recorded his first album with John Coltrane—*Miles*[44] for *Prestige*—and before the end of 1956 he completed his first *Columbia* album with the same quintet.[45]

The 1955 sessions, made in the year of Bird's death, once again set standards of excellence. These records, which introduced John Coltrane with Miles, may have been as significant to the young jazz musicians of the mid 1950s as Bird's *Savoy* recordings had been a decade earlier to Miles's generation.

The Davis rhythm section from 1956 to 1958 was known as just that—"the rhythm section"—and appeared as such on an Art Pepper record.[46] They were pianist Red Garland, bassist Paul Chambers, and virtuoso drummer Rudolph "Philly Joe" Jones. who played sporadically with Davis from 1952-58, and later led his own small groups.

Davis's affiliation with *Columbia* led to important recordings with arranger Gil Evans in 1957[47] and 1958.[48] The drummer for the *Miles Ahead* session is the swinging Arthur Taylor, and "Philly Joe" Jones plays the *Porgy and Bess* session, where his solo fills on the track "Gone" are modern jazz drumming classics.

---

[42]*A Night At Birdland* in 2 volumes Art Blakey (2/21/54) Blue Note B21Y-46519 and B21Y-46520
  At The Cafe Bohemia in 2 volumes Art Blakey (11/11/55) Blue Note B21Y-46521 and B21Y-46522
  Ritual Art Blakey (2/11/57) Blue Note B21Y-46858
  Moanin' Art Blakey (10/30/58) Blue Note B21Y-46516
  Mosaic Art Blakey (10/2/61) Blue Note B21Y-46523

[43]*The Complete Savoy Recordings Of Charlie Parker* Charlie Parker, Savoy (4 CD box ZDS 5500)

[44] *Miles* Prestige OJCCD-005-2, also in *Chronicle, the Complete Prestige Recordings* 8PRCD 012-2

[45]*'Round Midnight* Miles Davis (10/27/55) Columbia LP 1020 and CD CK 40610

[46]*Art Pepper Meets The Rhythm Section* Art Pepper (1/19/57) Contemporary OJCCD 338-2

[47]*Miles Ahead* Miles Davis (5/6/57) Columbia LP 1041 and CD CK 40784

[48]*Porgy and Bess* Miles Davis (7/22/58) Columbia LP 1274 and CD CK 40647

21

In 1959 the famous recording *Kind Of Blue* [49] introduced Bill Evans and Wynton Kelly as Miles Davis's pianists, and Jimmy Cobb as his drummer. Cobb stayed with Davis until 1963, when Tony Williams became the drummer. Jimmy Cobb always provides strong swinging accompaniment and exciting, cleanly articulated cadential solos.

Alto saxophonist Julian "Cannonball" Adderly, touted by some as the new Bird, was featured along with John Coltrane on *Kind of Blue*. In addition to being a lyric masterpiece, the recording introduced the concept of "modalism" to jazz of the '60s. Essentially, this is the use of one mode at a time (or a combination of related modes) to serve as an alternative reference for the improviser. By using this system, where vertical harmony is secondary to broader horizontally related tonalities, more direct linear development results. This innovative concept led to compositions and performances of the '60s where even broader harmonic/modal formats were used. The impact on drumming styles of the sixties is discussed in the next chapter.

John Coltrane's playing had developed during his tenure with Miles, and in 1960 he formed and recorded his own quartet. [50] The exciting group included pianist McCoy Tyner and drummer Elvin Jones, who stayed with him into 1965 to make more jazz history. Miles continued his own contributions to jazz history through 1992, the year of his death.

Modern jazz drumming of the 1950s was characterized by excellent musicianship and swinging accompaniment. Diverse musical styles called for continued flexibility and musical knowledge. As in the decades before—until the mid '50s—supportive (mostly non- broken) time playing prevailed, although in the new bop style.

Independent coordination, which had become a necessary technique for earlier bop drumming of the late '40s and early '50s, slowly changed to a more linear approach suited to the music of the late '50s and early '60s. Independence, in its pure form, is contrary to linear integration (melodies combining different instruments of the set without necessarily riding the cymbal).

In the late fifties Elvin Jones, Pete LaRoca, and Billy Higgins began to play more freely with cymbal phrases. Other drummers followed. Their breakaway evolved, in part, because of the difficulty required to sustain independent voices simultaneously. By 1960 independent drumming, which began as an alternative to conservative dance drumming styles, had become ineffectual because of its own stringent limitations.

The end of the fifties marked a major turning point for jazz and jazz drumming, which would be developed in the next decade by two groups whom I call the late modernists and the avant-garde. Some players belonged to both groups, and others held varying degrees of preference for playing "free".

---

[49] *Kind Of Blue* Miles Davis (3/2/59) Columbia LP1355 and CD CK 40579
[50] *My Favorite Things* John Coltrane   (10/21/60) Atlantic LP1361 and CD 1361-2
  Coltrane Plays The Blues John Coltrane (10/24/60) Atlantic LP1382 and CD 1382-2
  Coltrane's Sound John Coltrane   (10/24/60) Atlantic LP1419 and CD 1419-2

Late Modernism/The Avant-Garde (1960-1970)

Freer styles were developing while John Coltrane was still with the Miles Davis band in the late fifties. *Giant Steps*[51]—Coltrane's pinnacle of modern jazz harmony—is considered by some to have been his last recording to embrace extensive vertical harmony. It featured drummers Arthur Taylor and Jimmy Cobb (Lex Humphries played in an alternate session). Later in the same month of May 1959, Ornette Coleman recorded *The Shape of Jazz to Come*,[52] which suggested a freer harmonic approach. As its title accurately indicates, other jazz musicians began to explore looser formats for their music. *The Shape of Jazz to Come* and Coleman's second *Atlantic* album, prophetically titled *Change of the Century*,[53] both featured drummer Billy Higgins.

John Coltrane formed his quartet in 1960 immediately after his five year tenure with Davis's Quintet. Elvin Jones joined him that year to complete the new quartet, making it a major voice for the new music of the 1960s. In 1962 Jimmy Garrison became the bassist, and the quartet stayed together into 1965 when Jones and pianist McCoy Tyner left. Until his death in 1967 Coltrane experimented with other groups, but his music developed most significantly within his quartet (and quintet with Eric Dolphy) with Elvin Jones. Largely because of Elvin's original concepts and innovations, the quartet attained amazing levels of sustained improvisation. I remember watching Elvin (at the *Half Note)* sweating profusely as endings were extended for many minutes.

As in previous decades, drumming in the '60s was, to some extent, directed by the styles initiated by other instruments. Now, however, musical styles encouraged assertive drum accompaniment. This was due, in part, to the simpler and more minimal melodic and/or harmonic activity found in the compositions of the '60s. The static modal harmonies, like those favored by Coltrane in his post *Giant Steps* period, naturally led to a more democratic participation from drummers.

The subdominant role of the piano also provided new opportunities for dominant drumming styles. McCoy Tyner, Coltrane's pianist, often would stroll (rest) for long periods during Coltrane's solos. The bassist would do the same—leaving Elvin and Coltrane to play an exciting duet. Ornette Coleman chose not to use piano at all in his quartet of alto sax (and later violin), pocket trumpet, bass, and drums.

Free jazz and free jazz drumming were closely linked to the movement for racial equality and social justice. Strong African American leadership came from men like Dr. Martin Luther King Jr. and Malcolm X. The courage they demonstrated gave new hope of change to all Americans in the 1960s. Authentic African American jazz drumming had been waiting for this moment ever since slave owners banned drums generations earlier. The time was right for change and for Elvin Jones, whose style was the prototype of liberated jazz drumming.

---

[51] *Giant Steps* John Coltrane (5/4&5/59) Atlantic LP1311 and CD 1311-2

[52] *The Shape of Jazz to Come* Ornette Coleman (5/22/59) Atlantic CD 1317-2; Rhino box R271410

[53] *Change of the Century* Ornette Coleman (10/8/59) Atlantic CD 81341- 4; Rhino box R271410

Elvin Jones was the first drummer to introduce total linear integration of all the voices of the drum set. His new steps led the way, in a major phase of modern jazz drumming, during an experimental period of jazz after 1960. Following his lead, young jazz drummers promptly began to experiment with "rule breaking". Some conservative players (non- drummers) were not pleased with the freer styles. Other more experimental instrumentalists welcomed the fresh new face of drumming. As Roach had been the leader during the '50s, Elvin Jones and Tony Williams led jazz styles through the '60s.

We hear some of Elvin's breakthroughs even in his earlier recordings of the late '50s, before he joined John Coltrane. Especially exciting is the recording of a trio, without piano, led by Sonny Rollins at *The Village Vanguard* (11/3/57) which also introduced Pete LaRoca.[54] But it was Elvin's partnership with Coltrane that led him deeper into his development and set the pace for freer jazz styles. There is an extensive discography available of their live performances and studio dates on both *Atlantic* and *Impulse*.

The small set first used by Elvin Jones in the late '50s and later by Tony Williams in the early '60s became a popular jazz drum kit size:

Snare drum	5 or 5&1/2 x14
Small tom-tom	8x12
Floor tom-tom	14x14
Bass drum	14x18

Although not all players used this set up, wood shelled drums of these sizes made by the Gretsch Drum Company became the "classic" modern jazz model of the 1960s. The small wood Gretsch kit was the '60's version of Gene Krupa's classic Slingerland *Radio Kings* of the '40s. Even though Jones and Williams popularized the tom-tom-like 14x18 inch bass drum, 14x20 and 14x22 drums remained standard sizes.

Jones and Williams both used K. Zildjian cymbals made in Istanbul. Their rich, dark tones identify each drummer's special signature sound. The Zildjian family in America, who had supplied Chick Webb, Buddy Rich, Dave Tough, Jo Jones, and all the great swing drummers, continued to produce fine instruments in the Boston area. In the '60s Paiste, of Switzerland, began to distribute their cymbals in America. Roy Haynes and Marty Morell both recorded with Paiste flat ride cymbals in the mid to late '60s.

Billy Higgins and Ed Blackwell, each with his own special style, were musical leaders within the early Ornette Coleman quartets. Higgins's approach was strong but minimal, giving Coleman's music leanness and transparency. He played ensemble heads in a lightly outlined unison with the horns, and his crisp attack and thoughtful solos always complimented Coleman's exciting new music. Billy Higgins remains an outstanding drummer whose musicianship is renown. His large discography represents an impressive variety of important modern jazz recordings of more than three decades.

---

[54] *A Night at the Village Vanguard* (2 vols.) Sonny Rollins, Blue Note CDs: B21Y-46517; B21Y-46518

Ed Blackwell (1929-1992), a New Orleans drummer, was a more aggressive soloist. He played an extraordinary drum solo on the tune "T and T"[55] with Coleman's quartet, where his use of African polyrhythms is reminiscent of earlier New Orleans master drummer Warren "Baby" Dodds. Both Higgins and Blackwell played together in a double quartet on *Free Jazz*.[56] Danny Richmond was the favorite drummer of Charles Mingus, whose music is representative of the African American liberation movement in the '60s. Richmond's enthusiastic drumming compliments Mingus's special brand of composition and ensemble style. Other late modernists who represent the '60s are Joe Chambers, Pete LaRoca, Paul Motian, Albert Heath, Ben Riley, Walter Perkins, Roy Brooks, Frank Dunlop, Jimmy Lovelace, Clifford Jarvis, Freddie Waits, Dennis Charles and J.C Moses.

None of these musicians, however, had nearly the impact on future drumming styles as Anthony (Tony) Williams. His debut recording with the Miles Davis quintet in 1962 presents bold new ideas and solos which represent the continuation of Elvin Jones's innovations.[57] An admirer of Boston's Roy Haynes and student of another important '60s drummer, Alan Dawson, Williams joined Miles Davis's quintet in 1963 and remained into 1969. During that time his creative drumming style matured to make him a leader of jazz drumming trends of the '60s. Almost all jazz drummers of the '60s were influenced by his innovations. They eagerly awaited Miles's latest album to see what Tony would try next. Many of his new ideas were quickly accepted and emulated by Jack DeJohnette, Marty Morell, Lenny White, Steve Gadd, and a new generation of drummers whose careers developed in the '70s.

The avant-garde movement, led by disciples of Coltrane and Coleman, found its center in NYC. Saxophonists Archie Shepp and Albert Ayler led controversial free jazz groups which included outstanding drummers Andrew Cyrylle, Sonny Murray, Milford Graves, Beaver Harris, and Coltrane's last drummer, Rashid Ali. These exciting groups were predominantly African American. They tended to be generally exclusive—with few white members, particularly drummers. This was understandable because of their participation in the black liberation movement. These artists forged another important chapter of jazz development—early "free jazz". But unlike early bop (modernism), early free jazz (avant-garde) did not inspire a major developmental period. Neo-free music can often to be conspicuously uninteresting, while its predecessor of the '60s was sometimes brilliant.

At the same time, white British rock bands were becoming heroes in the US, which accounts for part of the decline of national jazz popularity. Changing social movements in North America needed new musical symbols to represent emerging attitudes. The new popular music, rock and roll, became—and may remain, in mutated forms—the banner of young Americans in their effort to identity themselves. Young audiences were listening to *The Jimi Hendrix Experience*, *Sly & The Family Stone*, *The Jefferson Airplane*, Bob Dylan, and others whose lyrics spoke to sexual, social, and political issues. The most important theme became resistance to the Vietnam war (1964-1973).

---

[55] *Ornette* Ornette Coleman (1/31/61) Atlantic LPSD1378; 6 CDbox, Rhino R271410
[56] *Free Jazz* Ornette Coleman (12/21/60) Atlantic LPSD1364; CD1364-2; 6 CDbox ,Rhino R271410
[57] *Seven Steps to Heaven* Miles Davis (4/16/63) Columbia LP CL 2501 and CD CK 48827

Through the mid '60s jazz drummers remained generally unaffected by the growing electronic revolution, but as the '70s approached, acoustic music deferred to emerging fusion styles. There were major equipment changes directly due to the increased dynamic levels of popular music. Plastic tipped sticks were used. As guitar and keyboard amplifiers became larger and louder, so did drum equipment. Curiously, the front heads were removed from bass drums for this purpose. Although this change gives a more direct projection of attack and allows microphone placement inside the drum, it actually diminishes the drum's natural full sound. Bottom tom-tom heads were sometimes removed as well. Even though this equipment was used primarily by non-jazz drummers of the '60s, the changes have influenced the sound of all drumming. It has affected the way that drummers hear themselves and their recordings.

A Post Script (1970 and beyond)

By the late 1960s popular jazz/rock styles had almost completely taken over the "cutting edge" that had belonged to late modernists and the avant-garde earlier in the decade. Miles Davis continued to set the pace for the '70s. *Bitches Brew*, recorded in 1969, was a pivotal recording which forecast the shape of jazz/fusion styles for the next two decades. One of the drummers for the date was Jack DeJohnette, who joined Miles in 1969 and stayed until mid-1972. Billy Cobham, Jack's replacement, played also with *The Mahavishnu Orchestra* which, like *Weather Report* and *Return to Forever,* began early in the decade, peaked near the middle, and declined by the '80s.

Natural acoustic properties of drum equipment after 1970 were altered. Oil-filled drum heads mute the drum's natural resonance. Roto tom-toms are merely drum heads on rims, with no drum shell whatsoever. Most bass drums used today have a six inch hole in the center of the front head. Calf heads, Turkish cymbals, and small wooden Gretsch drums are still available, but are rare and expensive.

There have been some exciting developments in the area of electronics. Drum synthesis calls for knowledge of technology and compositional skills, which some drummers use successfully as an extension of their instrument.

I notice a critical difference between digital and analog re-mastered recordings (LPs). Digital recording is often high-ended, with little, if any, warmth to the lower range of bass drum or cymbal overtone. This lack of representation is unfortunate, as it omits the essence of what the musicians were trying to achieve in the first place—ambience.

Classic American jazz has its future in the hands of young musicians such as the Marsalis brothers, and in the efforts of others who are preserving the musical legacy through recording and performance—David Baker and Gunther Schuller's *Smithsonian Jazz Masterworks* series, Larry Ridley's *Jazz Legacy Ensemble*, John Lewis at Cooper Union, and institutions that have initiated educational programs to ensure a future for the art. Kenny Washington, Bill Stewart, and other young drum masters are our links to jazz drumming in the twenty-first century.

Kenny Clarke

Kenneth Spearman Clarke (Liaquat Ali Salaam)   born Pittsburgh, PA 1/9/14
                                                 died Montrieuil, France 1/26/85

"Klook" is the drummer who perfectly bridged the swing styles of the '30s to the modern movement of the '40s. He had begun experimenting with drum accompaniment patterns as early as 1935, the year he moved to NYC from his hometown of Pittsburgh. Regarding his innovations, Clarke said that they were part of the natural evolution of the development of drumming. Having noticed the bass violin's changing role in the mid '30s, he began to carefully modify his drumming style, keeping time on a cymbal while playing less continuously on the bass drum. This single step liberated the use of bass drum and snare drum from then on. Though he often encountered resistance from the more conservative players with whom he worked, Clarke persisted with his ideas. His monumental contributions make him the "father of modern jazz drumming". It is interesting that such profundity was built upon simple logical criteria, both musical and physical. His innovations were finally accepted, and by 1945 others continued to develop the style which he introduced. Drummers of the next generation, including Billy Higgins and Louis Hayes, have acknowledged his influence on their styles.

Clarke also played trombone, piano, and mallet instruments. "Epistrophy" and "Salt Peanuts" are two of his compositions. Such broad musical knowledge likely contributed to his vision of drumming. He is well known for his superb accompaniment to many jazz artists, so that during the 1950s and '60s he was one of the most recorded drummers. His extensive discography displays incomparable consistency.

Subtle use of stick timbre, where the sticks carry the sound as much as the instrument struck, is a characteristic heard on many Clarke recordings. He often used a stick-over-stick technique (sometimes called "stickshots") favored by the swing drummers. His snare drum sound was identifiable for its deep and resonant tone. Subtle brush sweeps were another of his trademarks—he sometimes used a brush on his snare and a stick on the cymbal—or reversed position, playing opposite instruments.

But his renowned ride cymbal sound was his most famous signature. A medium size ride cymbal was mounted on his bass drum in a low, flat (non-tilted) position. His ride cymbal lines can be described as "horizontal"—not necessarily accenting the second and fourth beats. The notes are balanced and gracefully placed, in a straight quarter note pattern. Often his ride cymbal line would either pause for a beat to accommodate an accompaniment figure played by the snare and/or bass drum, or double the figure (that is, as a double stop, or unison) with his cymbal. Max Roach, commenting on Clarke's technique of playing straight quarters on the cymbals, once asked, "Many drummers play quarter notes on their ride cymbal, but how many make the notes dance like Kenny does?"

During the latter half of his life, which was spent almost entirely in France, Kenny Clarke was an important educator. He and teacher Dante Augostini founded a school for drummers in Paris. While in Europe, Arthur Taylor also taught there.

Kenny Clarke Timeline

EARLY DAYS IN PITTSBURGH 1914-35

Comes from a musical family
Studies piano, trombone, xylophone, drums, and music theory
Travels to the Midwest with bands in the early '30s
Plays drums with Roy Eldridge in Pittsburgh 1935

NY MOVE, Late 1935

Moves to NYC with brother Frank (bass player) and both join
Lonnie Simmons sextet which includes guitarist Freddie Green
They play at Greenwich Village club, *The Black Cat* in 1936

EDGAR HAYES, 1st EUROPE TRIP '37-'38

3/9/37	NYC, first Hayes recordings (see G. Schuller's *Swing Era* p. 421)
Late '37/Early '38	European tour with Hayes orchestra
3/8/38	Stockholm, first record as leader *Kenny Clarke Kvintett*

TEDDY HILL, NYC 1938-39

1938	Joins Hill's band which includes Dizzy Gillespie
	Dizzy encourages him to try his new ideas
1939	Hill fires Klook because of experimental drumming

PRE-*MINTON'S* PERIOD, NYC 1940-41

2/5/40	Records with Sidney Bechet
5/15/40	Records with Mildred Bailey (Roy Eldridge)
9/12/40 & 3/21/41	Records with Billie Holiday (Lester Young)
5/21/41	Records with Count Basie
Summer '41	Tour with Louis Armstrong
Autumn '41	Tour with Ella Fitzgerald's Chick Webb band (Dizzy Gillespie)

MINTON'S NYC 1941-43

Leads house band at Harlem after hours club until drafted into the army in mid-1943. Band includes Thelonious Monk, Dizzy Gillespie, Don Byas, and guitarist Charlie Christian

2nd EUROPE TRIP 1943-46 (In the Army)

Stationed in Normandy where he meets pianist John Lewis
Not active as a drummer at this time

RETURN TO NYC 1946-47

1946	Marries singer Carmen McRae
1946	Converts to Islam (changes name to Liaquat Ali Salaam)
5/15/46	Records with Dizzy's sextet: Al Haig, Milt Jackson, S. Stitt, R. Brown
6/10/46	Records with Dizzy's big band, becomes regular member (8 mos.)
9/5/46	Records with own group *Kenny Clarke and His 52nd Street Boys*
1946-47	Many more important recordings made during this period

3rd EUROPE TRIP 1948 (Gillespie big band)
Late winter 1948   Tour ends in Early Spring
Early spring 1948   Remains in France- plays and records with own groups

RETURN TO NYC 1948-49
1948-49   Joins Tadd Dameron's sextet, radio brodacasts from *Royal Roost*
4/21/49   Records with Tadd Dameron for *Capitol*
4/22/49   Records with Miles Davis nonet for *Capitol*

4th EUROPE TRIP 1949-51, PARIS JAZZ FESTIVAL
5/8/49   Appears with Miles Davis at Paris jazz festival, then stays in Paris
                         Records there with Europeans and visiting American musicians

RETURN TO NYC 1951-56
8/8/51   Records with Charlie Parker for *Mercury*
5/9/51   Records with Miles Davis for *Blue Note*
12/22/52   Records with *MJQ* for *Prestige*—stays with them till 1955
4/29/54   Records with Miles Davis for *Prestige* (*Walkin'* session)
1954-56   On staff at *Savoy* [58]
1955-56   Continues active recording career with Monk, "Cannonball", others

5th (final) EUROPE TRIP 1956
Early autumn '56   Arrives in Paris—makes France his permanent home

During late '50s   Continues jazz recordings, but more minimally
                    Remarries and has a son (his second)
                    Becomes an active teacher

LAST YEARS 1960-85
1961-72   Co-leads an international big band with pianist, Francy Boland
1956-84   Appears in European jazz festivals
1/26/85   Dies in Montrieuil France

Thanks to Mike Hennessey for his informative book "Klook", which I recommend for additional discography information. Thanks also to my friend Michael Haggerty who is responsible for organizing the extensive Kenny Clarke discography.

---

[58] The following Japanese (*Denon*) *Savoy* CDs are recommended: Telefunken Blues SV- 0106, Bohemia After Dark SV- 0107, Presenting Cannonball SV-0108, Opus de Jazz SV-0109, MJQ SV-0111, Nica's Tempo SV-0126, Wilder 'N Wilder SV-0131, Do It Yourself Jazz SV-0130, Byrd's Word SV-0132, The Jazz Message of Hank Mobley vol.1 SV-0133, The Jazz Message of Hank Mobley vol.2 SV-0158, Jay & Kai SV-0163, The Jazz Skyline SV-0173, All About Ronnie SV-0174, Jackson'sville SV- 0175, Jazzmen Detroit SV-0176, The Jazz Trio of Hank Jones (The Trio/Kenny Clark) SV-0184

Max Roach

Roach, Maxwell   born New Land, NC 1/10/24

It is difficult to identify Max Roach on his earliest 1944 recordings as a sideman in Benny Carter's big band, where he demonstrates accompaniment of restraint and finesse in the tradition of the great swing drummers, especially with his Jo Jones-like hi-hat style. However, sometimes his playing with the Carter band is similar to Art Blakey's early work with Billy Eckstine's band of the same period. Both use strong bass drum anticipations to support ensemble figures—sometimes filling in between them with tom-toms or stick shots on the snare drum.

A Charlie Parker session for *Savoy* (11/26/45) introduced Roach as an equal member of the ensemble. The classic session was brief as he points out in the following excerpt from a 1988 interview: "There was the record ban on and we had to get a whole album done in three hours".[59] His drumming on the recording demonstrates authoritative commentary in active dialogue with the others in the quintet.

 It seems to me that such playing was contingent on his command of solo skills. That is, even though he was not soloing in a literal sense, his "drum track" was a complete composition independent from the rest of the ensemble, yet complimentary to it. So, if the rest of the group had stopped at any point, he could have continued to complete the performance with no lack of interest. This situation did, in fact, once happen on a recorded performance.[60]

In the same 1988 interview, his view of his own playing during that period is somewhat different: "Not only using the drums as an accompanying instrument, which is mainly what I did with Charlie Parker and those folks, but now finding a way for the instrument to communicate with people on its own terms. I knew it could be done. The great African drummers do it, of course. But my approach came out of working with Charlie Parker, my desire to be on the front line, to be the lead as they are. 1949—from that point on I started dealing with the instrument seriously as a solo instrument that could become as prominent and valid artistically as any other instrument."[61]

The following are some of his many accomplishments :

Sideman and band leader to many other jazz masters

Solo drum set recitalist

Educator

Composer/leader of percussion, string, choral, and jazz ensembles

---

[59] Pulse magazine interview 12/88, Gene Santoro
[60] "Un Poco Loco" #2 *The Amazing Bud Powell* vol.1 Bud Powell (5/1/51) Blue Note CD B21Y-81503
[61] Pulse magazine interview 12/88, Gene Santoro

The Un Poco Loco Sequence

The 1951 "Un Poco Loco" session, with Bud Powell and Curly Russell for *Blue Note,* [62] includes three different versions of Powell's classic composition in performance order. These tracks offer insight into the compositional prowess of both Powell and Roach.

Take #1—After an eight measure introduction, the 64 measure head, which is in 16 bar units (AABA), is played. Roach chooses a standard mambo beat (reverse clave) on a cow bell to accompany Powell's melody, which is based on a frontward clave pattern. The same bell pattern, with slight variation, is sustained during Powell's solo until the end of the piece. Without a return to the melody of the head, this version ends abruptly after two measures of Roach's beat—played as a solo—since Powell had stopped.

Take #2—After the same introduction, Roach uses an entirely different bell pattern for both A sections of the head. The pattern, which is played within the sixteen eighth notes of a two measure phrase, outlines two groups of five notes and one group of six. This is a marvelous example of his command of polymetric phrasing. Roach plays the bridge similarly to the first take, but with slightly more development—using a cymbal to mark accents, and drum fills at the ends of phrases. Contrasting dynamics are used during the interlude; Roach plays the first six bars (of the interlude) in unison, lightly underlining Powell's attacks; the last two bars are fuller, with cymbal crashes supported by bass drum—then, it's back to the 5-5-6 bell ostinato for most of the remainder of the piece except for the drum solo, which may have come as a surprise to Roach. He doesn't waste time seizing the opportunity and introduces his solo with a cymbal crash, and then plays a brief, but fascinating, solo of 16 bars or so. He uses interesting rim sounds and muffling techniques on the snare drum with the snares off. As with an earlier session with Powell's trio for *Roost*, he uses a very basic set (no tom-toms heard). Powell returns with the head, but with no bridge this time. The interlude is used as an ending for both this version and the final take #3.

Take #3—This final take was used as the original master and was the first to be issued. The players seem more relaxed on this track. It is generally the same arrangement as take #2, except that in this version the entire head (including the bridge) is played during the out chorus. During the first bridge, Roach is less noticeable than before. He insinuates a trace of half time feel in bar 8 of the interlude by playing his rim on the pick-up beat (beat three). In his solo, Powell leaves more silence between his phrases. This highlights Roach's new bell pattern which he now begins to develop subtly. The drum notes which had earlier been somewhat anonymous "fill notes" now take on a more contrasting, linear function to the two bell notes of the still dominant bell ostinato. The new linear beat is counterpoint to Powell's figures; the result is extraordinary and at times hypnotic. Roach's twenty-two measures of solo is followed by a four bar cue, to which Powell does not respond until Roach plays another four bars of the ostinato.

---

[62] *The Amazing Bud Powell* vol.1 Bud Powell (5/1/51) Blue Note CD B21Y-81503

An earlier use of metric superimposition is heard on a 1949 Sonny Stitt quartet recording (again with Russell and Powell) of "I Want to Be Happy" [63] where Roach's ride cymbal patterns, along with Powell's accompaniment, suggest 3/4 meter.

In 1953, Roach was reunited with Charlie Parker for a quartet recording. This session provides fine examples of his drum solos from that period. The high pitches of his drums spell an F major arpeggio up from the floor tom tom. His bass drum keeps a steady 4/4 pulse while his hands play melodic phrases around the tom-toms and snare drum. There is interaction of his drumming with pianist Hank Jones's accompaniment patterns over Percy Heath's walking bass solo on the alternate take #2 of "Kim". [64]

From 1954-56 Roach led an important quintet with trumpeter Clifford Brown. It ended abruptly with the tragic deaths of two of his band members—Brown and pianist Ritchie Powell (younger brother of the great Bud Powell)—in an auto accident 6/26/56. There are excellent examples of Roach's extended solos on the records made by that classic group, which sometimes included Sonny Rollins. They recorded for *EmArcy*. [65]

His ability to participate with instrumental equality is heard on the 1957 J.J.Johnson title, "Commutation", [66] where he plays one chorus of a drum solo accompanied by a walking bass line. After that, he and J.J.Johnson trade fours for 16 bars, then twos at the bridge, and ones for the first 16 bars of the next chorus. The next bridge is a bowed bass solo which he accompanies. During all these events there is such smoothness and flow to his playing that it might go by without particular notice, unless you are a drummer. He seems to play the drums as he would a melodic instrument.

During the late 1950s and the early '60s Roach became an activist and leader in the African American liberation movement. Some of his recordings during this period reflect this. He continued to lead his own quintets, but as of 1957 he discontinued using a pianist as a regular group member, although he has recorded several duet albums with pianists over the years. He has been featured on numerous recordings as a special guest with artists such as George Russell[67] and Thelonious Monk.[68] His solos on the Monk album are in choruses, again melodic-like drum lines. More recently he has performed his own unaccompanied solo concerts and recitals.

He has written many original compositions in odd meters including 3/4, 5/4, and 7/4. His ensemble members were some of the first to improvise convincingly in these meters. "A Man from Africa", recorded in 1961, is his blues line in seven.[69] An earlier 1956 quintet recording *Jazz in 3/4 Time* was played exclusively in waltz time.[70]

---

[63] *Sonny Stitt / Bud Powell / J.J.Johnson* Sonny Stitt (1/26/50) Prestige OJCCD-009-2

[64] *Now's the Time/The Genius of C.P.* Charlie Parker (7/30/53) Verve LP MGV8005 and CD 825671-2

[65] *Brownie: The Complete recordings of Clifford Brown* 10 CD box EmArcy 838 306-2

[66] *First Place* J.J. Johnson (5/12/57) Columbia LP JLC 1030

[67] *New York,New York* George Russell (9/12/58) Decca CD MCAD 31371

[68] *Brilliant Corners* Thelonious Monk (10/15/56) Riverside OJCCD-026-2

[69] *Percussion Bitter Sweet* Max Roach (8/1/61) Impulse CD GRP GRD122

[70] *Jazz in 3/4 Time* Max Roach (3/18/57) Mercury LP MG36108

Max Roach Timeline

CHILDHOOD Family moves to NY in 1928—played in bands in his late teens

EARLY CAREER

Early '40s	Attends Manhattan School of Music
1942	First association with Bird
2/44	First record with Coleman Hawkins *Apollo*
5/21/44	West coast tour and recording with Benny Carter *Capitol* LP M-11057
1944	Joins Dizzy Gillespie small group on 52nd street

WITH CHARLIE PARKER 1945-1950 (late '49)

5/25/45	First record with Bird (Sarah Vaughn)*Spotlite* (UK) LP SPJ 150
11/26/45	First *Savoy* recording session with Bird, Diz, Miles *Savoy* CD SV-0105
1946	Bird leaves for west coast with Dizzy's band (drummer is Stan Levey)
1946	Active in NYC
1/10/47	Records with Bud Powell trio *Roost, Roulette* CD B21Y 93902
1947	Bird returns to NYC, Max joins band
5/8/47	Second *Savoy* record with Bird, Miles, Powell *Savoy* CD SV-0104
10/28/47	Records with Bird *Dial,* Four CD box *Stash* STCD 567/8/9/10
1948	Broadcasts from *Royal Roost* with Bird *Savoy* CDs SV-0155, SV-0156
4/5/49	Records with Bird *Mercury (Clef)* incl.in *Bird,* 10 CD box*Verve* 10-837141
5/49	Trip to France with Bird *Paris Jazz Festival*

ACTIVITY IN NYC 1950-54

1/17/51	Records with Bird and Miles *Mercury (Clef)* incl. in *Bird ,Verve* 10 CD box
5/1/51	Records with Bud Powell (Un Poco Loco) *Blue Note* CD B21Y 81503
5/10/53	First record *M.R. Quartet featuring Hank Mobley Debut* OJCCD-202-2
5/15/53	Massey Hall concert (Toronto) Bird, Diz, Powell, Mingus OJCCD-044-2
1954	California trip, recordings with west coast jazz musicians OJCCD-154-2

LEADS OWN GROUPS from 1954

WITH CLIFFORD BROWN 1954-56

Spring '54	Forms first group with Clifford Brown
1954-56	Several recordings *Brownie: The Complete EmArcy* 10CD box 838306-2
6/22/56	Records with Sonny Rollins quartet *Saxophone Colossus* OJCCD-291-2
6/26/56	Clifford Brown and Ritchie Powell die in an auto accident

WITH KENNY DORHAM, SONNY ROLLINS or HANK MOBLEY 1956-58

1956-57	Records *Max Roach Plus Four* (*& more*), EmArcy CD 822673-2
1957-8	Records quartets without pianist LPs: *EmArcy* MG 36127, *Argo* 623

WITH BOOKER LITTLE 1958-61

8/17/58	Records with *The Boston Percussion Ensemble*—EmArcy MG 36144
1960s	Marries Abbey Lincoln
8/31/60	Records *Freedom Now Suite*—*Candid* CD 9002
8/1/61	Records *Percussion Bittersweet*—*Impulse* GRP CD GRD-122
1961	Writes, records *It's Time* (includes vocal choir)*Impulse* (J)CDWMC5-121

LEADS VARIOUS GROUPS 1960-77

1964	Records *Max Roach trio with the Legendary Hassan*—*Atantic* CD782283
1965	Records *Drums Unlimited* (Freddie Hubbard) *Atlantic* (J) CD AMCY-1043
1968	European tour with Abbey Lincoln
1970	Percussion ensemble *M'Boom* is formed (later records for *CBS*)
1971	Records *Lift Every Voice* (includes vocal choir)*Atlantic* LP SD 1587

WITH CECIL BRIDGEWATER 1977-'90s

1/21/77	*Tokyo Concert Denon* TX -7508-ND

VARIOUS SPECIAL PROJECTS

8/30/77	Records an unaccompanied album *Solos* (Japan)*Baystate* LP RVJ-6021
10/19/84	Swedenbörg String Quartet, *Live at Vielharmonie Munich* SN 1073
11/2/84	*M'boom* records for *Soulnote* SN 1059CD
1/4/85	Record the double (string) quartet album, *Easy Winners* SN 1109
3/23/89	Duet concert and recording with Dizzy Gillespie (France) *A&M* CD6404
1991	Guest soloist at the funeral for dancer and choreographer, Alvin Ailey
1959-'90s	Holds teaching posts at Lenox School of Jazz and U Mass., Amherst

Quotes from Max

PHILOSOPHY " I always felt that the technique and knowledge of how to create form—in other words, how to take music and look at it architecturally—is the key to the drums. You build."

"There's a thin line between being a great creative artist and being a very successful popular artist. One does entertainment, and the other will live in his art. People are still feeding off what folks like Art Tatum did, piano players are still in awe of him; Charlie Parker, same thing; Dizzy, same thing; Miles, same thing. What I am came from a lot of people. I'm standing on a lot of shoulders; everybody is. Kenny Clarke and Papa Jo and Sidney Catlett and Gene Krupa and Buddy Rich and Art Blakey, all these folks you kinda gather on the inside, and what you play is representative of that."[71]

---

[71] Pulse Magazine interview 12/88, Gene Santoro

Roy Haynes

Roy Owen Haynes   born Roxbury, MA 3/13/26

Roy Haynes remains one of the most popular modern jazz drummers in the music business. This is due to his outstanding skills as an accompanist and his unique signature style and sound. Though difficult to describe, his style may have been the first major exposition of what we now call broken rhythms. That is, by using rests, or editing notes out of a phrase, the remaining notes suggest more rhythmic clarity. The effect of his confident phrasing is an outlining of notes as if printed in bold type. He is known for using "even" eighth notes in phrasing both his ride cymbal and drum accompaniment patterns. Analysis of his style reveals the use of simple rhythms in a syncopated polymetric fashion. This polymetric phrasing was a characteristic common to the bebop melodies of Bud Powell, Charlie Parker, and Miles Davis, with whom Haynes worked during the late 1940s.

In a description of his own playing, Haynes once referred to his internal time concept, which, he said, was common to other major jazz artists. He was one of first drummers to break up time with his hi-hat—especially in the late '50s and early '60s, when looser dialogue between ensemble players was becoming popular. He brought his unique style to the John Coltrane quartet, as Elvin Jones's temporary replacement in the early '60s.[72]

During that same period, saxophonist Stan Getz said that Haynes was his favorite drummer. From then to the present, he has recorded with many contemporary pianists, including Andrew Hill, McCoy Tyner, and Chick Corea. His smooth, elegant brush work in trio context is always a pleasure to hear. He recorded with Gary Burton's quartet, and more recently with Pat Metheny.

One of his signature sounds is the snare drum, where his snares are kept taut against the bottom head. The head tension is not necessarily tight, but the tension of the snares is. Because of this tension, his snare drum accompaniment patterns have a staccato-like "popping" effect. Haynes used a piccolo snare drum in the '50s when he played with Charlie Parker.

His accompaniment moves the music forward in a gentle, yet assertive fashion. Use of double time, or partial double time, figures is another Roy Haynes trademark. Bass drum and snare drum accents sometimes occur just slightly ahead of the downbeat—a fraction of a beat (16th or 32nd note) early.

Haynes's solo trades are often unpredictable. Their polyrhythmic character quickly catches our attention as eighth note triplets are phrased in groups of four notes, in his eight bar trades with Steve Lacy and Charles Davis on Parker's "Donna Lee".[73] He sometimes features a particular instrument. It's the hi-hat on his twelve bar chorus after Ron Carter's bowed bass solo on Jacki Byard's blues line "Mrs. Parker of K.C." [74]

---

[72] *Coltrane at Newport '63* John Coltrane (7/7/63) Impulse GRP CD GRD-128

[73] *The Straight Horn of Steve Lacy* Steve Lacy (11/19/60) Candid CD 9007

[74] *Far Cry* Eric Dolphy (12/21/60) New Jazz OJCCD-400

Haynes established his voice early—in the late '40s—and has been polishing it ever since. He plays in all kinds of ensemble settings: big band, trio, strings, vocal—and styles: traditional, avant-garde, etc. His versatility and flexibility are extraordinary.

He has led and recorded his own small groups from time to time. Like Art Blakey's *Jazz Messengers*, his band, *The Hip Ensemble,* has included up-and-coming young jazz artists: saxophonists Frank Strozier, Gary Bartz, and Ralph Moore; pianists Ronnie Mathews, Kenny Barron, Stanley Cowell, and George Cables.

Haynes's approach was studied and applied by another important drummer who grew up in Roxbury MA—Anthony Williams.

Roy Haynes abbreviated discography/timeline to the late '60s

1944	Plays in Boston with Frankie Newton and Pete Brown
1945-47	Travels with Luis Russell band in NYC area (Moves to NYC)
1947-49	Plays, records with Lester Young (Birdland broadcast recording)
1949	Plays, records with Bud Powell (see p. 15, first par.)
1949-52	Plays, records with Charlie Parker *Bird at St.Nick's* OJCCD-041-2
1950s	Plays, records with Sonny Rollins *Sound of Sonny* OJCCD-092-2
1953	Plays, records with Bud Powell *Inner Fires—Electra Mus.*71009
1953-58	Plays, records with Sarah Vaughn *Mercury* and *EmArcy*
1958	Plays, records with Thelonious Monk *In Action* OJCCD-103-2
1960	Records with Booker Little and Scott LaFaro *Bainbridge* CD1041
1960s	Records with: John Coltrane, Eric Dolphy (see footnotes p.35); Stan Getz (strings) *Focus—Verve* CD 821 982-2; Chick Corea (see *Drummer Discography*); many others; and leads quartet *Hip Ensemble*
1970s	Records with ChickCorea, Art Pepper, others leads *Hip Ensemble*
1980-'90s	Continues performances and recording activity leads *Hip Ensemble*

Art Blakey

Art Blakey (Buhaina Abdullah Ibn)   born Pittsburgh, PA 10/11/19
                                                     died NYC 10/16/90

Art Blakey's impact on jazz has been tremendous, as evidenced by his extensive discography. "The Fire" of jazz drumming is the title given to him by Dizzy Gillespie. Since the early '40s, his high spirited accompaniment and infectious swing sparked many historic jazz ensembles. He led his own quintet (occasionally sextet), *The Jazz Messengers,* for more than four decades until his death in 1990. Like Miles Davis, Blakey's leadership was crucial to the early careers of numerous young jazz greats who found their musical voices under his tutelage.

When he was a teenager in Pittsburgh, Blakey played piano before making drumming his career choice. He was self taught—inspired by Sid Catlett, Chick Webb, and probably Kenny Clarke. Clarke, who was five years older than Blakey and also from Pittsburgh, moved to NY in 1935. In 1942 Blakey, too, played in NY—with Mary Lou Williams. Art's first major exposure and development came during his years with Billy Eckstine's all star big band (1944-47). Because of his commitment to swing he became a living legend of modern jazz during his fifty year career. He chose the Muslim name Buhaina Abdullah Ibn and became world renown as a band leader. Even at the end of his life in 1990, when he was nearly deaf, he remained an extraordinary "Jazz Messenger".

Of the contributions he made to modern jazz drumming, his unique use of rhythm and polyrhythms is unprecedented—a link to authentic African drumming. He was one of the first jazz drummers to use polyrhythms extensively—often using "straight" (even) eighth note rhythm figures to assure forward motion of the music—while employing triplet rhythms on his cymbal. Roy Haynes also uses these straight eighth notes, but in a way that is usually more congruent to the rhythm of his cymbal time. Blakey's rhythmic flexibility is close to that of Elvin Jones, although their styles are dissimilar. Like Jones, he frequently uses polyrhythmic devices in his solo construction. But as Jones might shift from one rhythm to another, Blakey, who generally prefers one rhythm group at a time, might sustain two or more different rhythms simultaneously.

His drumming, like that of Max Roach, stands alone as a compositional entity both in solo and ensemble format. Although there are many unique facets to his playing, a brief description is that his drumming style is constantly balanced in a state of relaxed tension so that even when startling bursts of notes are flailed, they occur within a relaxed perimeter. This is characteristic of all the great jazz drummers, but particularly so of Blakey, who spoke of relaxation as an important drumming discipline (see p.39).

He used dynamic contrast between his cymbal time and drum fill(s). Sometimes he would play a dramatic press roll crescendo all the way from *ppp* to *fff.* I've seen him literally standing up at the climax of such rolls. Another way he achieves a surprise effect is his use of a single attack on a drum, within the flow of time. It comes through like a punch on the snare, as a rim shot, or a boot from the bass drum.

Texturally, he was innovative by using different tones of his drums and rims. He used a technique which he may have borrowed from Africa—one stick presses into the drum while the other stick strikes it. The pressed stick changes its position on the drum to change pitch. Using this technique, Blakey simulates scales of notes, moving upward, downward, or both. In another version of this, he uses his elbow pressing into the snare drum (snares off) for a scalewise effect. One of his trademarks is a rattling sound, made when the stick underneath is very quickly shuttled back and forth between the one on top and the drum head. Another rattling technique is two sticks played together. He used both drums and rims to produce cadences as a signal for ensemble entrance.

Art Blakey's Jazz Messengers abbreviated discography/timeline

1942-44	Play with Mary Lou Williams *Kelly's Stable*, Fletcher Henderson
1944-47	Plays with Billy Eckstine *Savoy* CD ZDS 4401
1947	First *Blue Note Jazz Messengers* (octet) *New Sounds* B21Y84436
1953	Plays, records with Buddy DeFranco *Verve* CD (Japan) J28J 25112
1954	Leads *Jazz Messengers* at *Birdland* with Clifford Brown, Lou Donaldson, Horace Silver, Curly Russell (see footnotes p. 21)
1955-56	Co-leads *Jazz Messengers* with Horace Silver; band includes Kenny Dorham, Hank Mobley, Doug Watkins (see footnotes p. 21)
1956-57	*Art Blakey's Jazz Messengers* Jackie McLean, Johnny Griffin, Bill Hardman, Sam Dockery, Spanky DeBrest (see footnotes p. 21)
1958	*Art Blakey's Jazz Messengers* Lee Morgan, Benny Golson, Bobby Timmons, Jimmy Merritt (see footnotes p. 21)
1959	*Art Blakey's Jazz Messengers* Hank Mobley for Golson *At the Jazz Corner of the World* 2 vols. *Blue Note* (J) CDs TOCJ-4015,6
1959/60	*Art Blakey's Jazz Messengers* Wayne Shorter for Mobley *The Big Beat* (3/6/60) *Blue Note* CD B21Y-46400
1961-64	*Art Blakey's Jazz Messengers* Freddie Hubbard for Morgan, Cedar Walton for Timmons, add Curtis Fuller (see footnotes p. 21)
1964-66	*Art Blakey's Jazz Messengers* combinations—former members and Keith Jarret, Chuck Mangione, Frank Mitchell, ReggieWorkman.
1966-80	*Art Blakey's Jazz Messengers* various changing groups
1980-90	*Art Blakey's Jazz Messengers* Wynton, and Branford Marsalis, Bill Pierce, James Williams—then changing groups

Quotes from Art Blakey

MODERN DRUMMER 9/84, interviewer Chip Stern

CHICK WEBB'S IMPACT ON DRUMMING STYLES "Chick Webb was the master of syncopation. Other drummers were just time-keepers in the band-any band. Chick Webb would interpret the arrangements, and the next guy I heard do that was Klook (1937). Interpreting arrangements is so important. Chick brought the drums to the front as a leader. The band would have to follow *his* cues, and that's where he brought the drums up front. He had the best sounding black band in the country.....He was the first drummer to syncopate melodic figures off the pulse... His bass drum was almost as tall as he was, and that used to tickle me. And his foot—this is where I learned about controlling the music with the bass drum. When he was playing, no matter what the speed or the tempo of the tune, his foot never stopped."

KENNY CLARKE "The first time I saw Klook it was so amazing to me, because he had one big Chinese cymbal, a bass drum, and a snare—no sock cymbals, He just had his foot stomping on the floor—lead foot."

RELAXATION "Freedom without discipline is chaos; you have to have some discipline. Discipline means to relax—that's what it takes to play the drums. That's what Chick Webb taught me. That's the only teacher I ever had who taught me anything—him and Sid Catlett. ....All of these kids ought to get up there and watch old drummers, like Kenny Clarke. He ain't gonna bust his butt for nothin'. He'll be up there playing a long time, and all of them will be if they just learn to relax. You don't have to impress nobody. And I happen to know that drummers are like that."

DYNAMICS/USE OF THE SET "I mean dynamics are so important to the music as a whole—to making the music relaxed and exciting. Drummers have to understand their role in the band and how important each part of the kit is to the section sound. Like playing the bass drum: A lot of drummers today have no bottom. They talk about punctuating, but they don't keep that in there, and that bass drum is the basis of the whole thing."

CYMBALS "Every cymbal means something different to me; they're totally different instruments."

PLAYING AND RECORDING WITH MONK "There was real freedom. If you didn't play the drums, he'd get upset about it. And the way I played with him on records set a precedent for the drum style, because cats who played with him from then on had to play with him in that vein."

Note: My Berklee colleague, John Ramsay, has written a book due for publication soon: *Art Blakey's Jazz Messages* Manhattan Music Publications, CPP Media. John has listed specific recordings that he used for his transcriptions of Blakey's drumming.

Philly Joe Jones

Rudolph " Philly Joe" Jones

born Philadelphia, PA 7/15/23
died Philadelphia, PA 8/30/85

Not related to Elvin, and sometimes confused with "Papa" Jo Jones, "Philly Joe" Jones played in a style between the two. Even though his drumming was a continuation of modernism introduced by Clarke and Roach, it displays traditionalism as well. His teacher, Cozy Cole, and his one time employer, Buddy Rich, were both influential. Jones also credits Baby Dodds, Chick Webb, and Sid Catlett as inspirations to his unique approach.

Even though Jones began playing drums as a child, his career developed rather late. After serving in the Army in 1941, he drove a streetcar in Philadelphia. He played in Philadelphia with Dizzy Gillespie, John Coltrane, the Heath Brothers, Fats Navarro, and Ben Webster. Moving to NY in 1947, he played with Charlie Parker. In 1949 he moved to Washington, DC. Returning to NY in 1952, this time to stay, he worked with Miles Davis. In 1953 he joined a group led by Tadd Dameron, with which he recorded later that year, beginning a 10 year period of active recording. He studied for three years with Cozy Cole at his NYC school and in 1951 was the drummer for Buddy Rich's big band. He observed Rich's drumming techniques and applied some of them to his own more modern concept.

Like Rich, Jones was a virtuoso not lacking showmanship. I once saw him in action, circa 1960, at one of the legendary Monday night jam sessions at *Birdland.* Joe was in the audience and either wanted to play and/or was displeased with the drummer who was playing at that time. He jumped onto the band stand, grabbed the drummer's sticks away from him, then pushed him aside and started to play as the uninvited substitute for the remainder of the up tempo tune. While he played and soloed (splendidly) he re-tuned the entire set, including bass drum, with a drum key held in his left hand and a stick between his teeth. I remember, as I watched the spectacle, being grateful that I wasn't the other drummer. Upon completion of his breath-taking performance, he disappeared with an exit as abrupt as his arrival. Those of us who had witnessed the scene were left in awe, as if to ask, "Who was that masked man?" His flamboyant personality often expressed itself musically. One of the several records under his own name is *Blues for Dracula*, on which he parodies the voice of Bela Lugosi.

He was Miles' favorite drummer—and from 1955 to 1958 was with John Coltrane, Paul Chambers and Red Garland in the Davis quintet. Joe described some of his feelings about Miles Davis to *Down Beat* interviewer Sandy Davis (9/9/76): "It was the greatest and happiest experience I've ever had in music. It helped groom me, it helped open my ears. It even forced me to study more. When you're playing with giants like that, you have to study...it was music, music, music. And learning, always learning."

His first ensemble choice was big band, but neither circumstances nor economics permitted it, except for recordings. Consequently, his touring groups were usually quartet or quintet. From 1958, he performed and recorded as a leader. His band members included saxophonists Bill Barron, Dale Hillary, and Charles Davis; trumpeters Mike Downs, Tommy Turrentine, and Dizzy Reece; and bassists Paul Chambers, Larry Ridley, and Marc Johnson.

Since he was one of the most popular jazz drummers of the fifties and early sixties, his discography is extensive. He recorded debut albums for both Freddie Hubbard and Lee Morgan. His broad cymbal beat provided a comfortable accompaniment to those he played with. Musicians referred to his cymbal time as a "pocket", in which they were given maximum rhythmic freedom to play their phrases.

His virtuosic drum solos were elegant and concise. If we listen carefully, we notice a similarity of phrases in his solos from one recording to another. Sometimes the same pattern is played almost note for note in a four bar exchange. This is not a redundant aspect of his style, but rather a characteristic of his signature sound. Instead of remaining mere clichés, these phrases are trademarks which identify him and give him a repertory from which he combines ideas. His friend Bill Evans, who loved to play with him, once described to me how he perceived Joe's phrases. "Joe is one of the few drummers who has discovered how to put the drum "rudiments" together to make interesting musical phrases. It's how he puts them together that makes him special." Not being a drummer and not knowing what actual drum rudiments are, Evans still heard these simple basic units as rudiments. In effect, Joe organized his own language system built upon his own special rudiments.

He had a full repertoire of brush styles as well, and in 1968 wrote the first book dealing with the subject. *Brush Artistry*, published in England by the Premier Drum Company, has long been unavailable in the US. The following titles of patterns give us clues to his system: Smooth One—Palm Up—Trill—Tense—Tippin'—The Cup—Half and Half—Eyes—Shuffling it—Sweeping it—Fancy Fancy.

Jones played piano and did some arranging. Although not a formal school teacher himself, he was active giving advice and coaching younger drummers throughout his career. One of Joe's protegés, Vincent Ruggiero, was instrumental in helping him organize and transcribe his concepts. Ruggiero's students in Rochester NY—some of whom are still active—thus received valuable instruction about Jones's techniques.

One trademark of his drumming style is a rim tap hit on the fourth beat of each bar, as in the recording "Milestones" (see Drummer Discography). Another is polymetric phrasing of 3/4 in 4/4 meter. This is particularly noticeable when Jones comes out of a four bar exchange, accents beat one, and follows with an accent on four (tied over the measure to beat one of the next bar etc.). Ruggerio calls this sound a "wash", or sustaining of sound, on the semi-open hi-hat cymbals. These, and other classic Philly Joe phrases, are still used by drummers today.

Philly Joe Jones timeline to the late '60s

1940-47	Philadelphia gigs with visiting NYC musicians
1947	Plays with Charlie Parker in NYC
1949	Moves to Washington
1951	Drummer for Buddy Rich's big band
1952	Moves to NYC - works with Miles Davis
1953	Records with Davis and Bird (1/30/53)*Collectors' Items* OJCCD-071-2
1953	Records with Clifford Brown (9/15/53) *Memorial* OJCCD-017-2
1953	Plays, records with Elmo Hope (6/18/53) *Blue Note* B21Y84438
1955-58	Begins active recording period and joins the Miles Davis quintet *Chronicle, Complete Prestige Recordings* Miles Davis 8PRCD-012-2
1956	Records *'Round About Midnight* (6/5/56) M.D.*Columbia* CD CK40610
1958	Records with Bill Evans (12/15/58) *Everybody Digs B.E.* OJCCD-068-2
1958	Performed and recorded as a leader (see*Drummer Discograpy*)
1962	Records with Tadd Dameron (4/16/62)*The Magic Touch* OJCCD-143-2
1967	Tours and records with Bill Evans *California,Here I Come* (may be released as a *Verve* CD in 1994/5)
1967-69	Lives and teaches in London
1968	*Brush Artistry* published by Premier Drum Company, England
1969-72	Lives in Paris
1972	Returns to Philadelphia
1976	Plays with Bill Evans
1976-85	Lives in Philadelphia, sometimes leading a quartet

Quotes from Philly Joe

Feb./Mar 82 *Modern Drummer,* interviewer Rick Mattingly

INFLUENCE/AFFILIATION WITH OTHER MASTER DRUMMERS

"I used to go and listen to Baby Dodds. His ride cymbal would be a 15", and he'd control it, which is hard to do. He would ride on that little cymbal and play all those funny licks he used to play on an Indian tom. No sock cymbal. And he'd be swinging!"

"I always tell the students I'm working with to listen to recordings of the great jazz drummers. If they can find anything by the greats, then they can hear how the drums have moved from Chick Webb's time to today. You can go back there and hear something that is still played today. I do a lot of things that Chick Webb used to play years ago."

"Sid Catlett used to show me a lot of things. I learned so many different ways of playing the brushes from studying with Sid. He was a fabulous brush-man."

"Kenny Clarke was my guru. When I lived in Paris, I would hang out with him all the time."

"I was in Buddy Rich's band in 51. Buddy would play a big solo once a night, and the rest of the time he would direct the band, and even sing!"

"I used to go to Max's house in Brooklyn and he would help me. He is one of my favorites."

INSTRUMENT CONCEPTS

"I'm still studying the instrument. I can handle it, but I learn something every time I play. With my control of the instrument, I'll take chances. I'll try anything. If I dream up something while I'm playing, I'll attempt it, because if I mess up, I know how to get out of it. I'll keep trying it until I do it. A lot of things I play are right off the top of my head. Many times, as soon as a thought comes into my mind, it goes right to my hands. If I fluff it somehow, you never know it, but I'll know it. There are a few things I won't attempt on the stand because if I miss it, I won't be able to clean it up. So I work with it in the house until I get it under control, and then I'll start doing it on the stand. I'll do it every night until I really get it down. Attempting things is dangerous if you don't have some experience."

PLAYING CONCEPTS

"When I'm going to play someone else's music, I try to sit down at the piano and play through it. If I'm playing a tune, I really like to know it. I don't like to take a shot at playing a tune I don't know. I never do that with my group. I tell everybody in the group, "Listen, if you don't know the tune-don't play.""

Elvin Jones

Elvin Ray Jones   born Pontiac, MI 9/9/27

Elvin grew up in a musical household. His older brothers, Thad and Hank Jones, both jazz giants themselves, encouraged his early music activities. His mother played piano in a Baptist church and the three brothers sang in the choir. In his early teens Elvin, who was mainly self-taught, practiced many hours every day.

He began his professional career playing in Pontiac and Detroit, and continued playing during Army service (1946-49). After returning to Michigan he resumed his professional career working with his brother Thad, Kenny Burrell, Donald Byrd, Barry Harris and Pepper Adams. His acquaintance with Art Mardigan—drummer in Billy Mitchell's quintet—was an important influence. In 1956 he moved to NYC. There he recorded with J.J. Johnson's quintet, Donald Byrd's quintet, Miles Davis, and Sonny Rollins's trio.

His recording activity during this period (late '50s) demonstrates his influence on those players with whom he played as a sideman. My friend Al Francis (a wonderful vibist who was then playing regularly at the *Cafe Wha* sessions in Greenwich Village), described the experience of playing with Elvin. He told me that when he listened to Elvin play with the others at the session, it didn't sound quite right—like maybe the time wasn't together. But when he played his solo with Elvin accompanying, he said the feeling was wonderfully free—as if he could play almost anything. Belgian tenor player, Bobby Jaspar, once compared playing with Elvin to riding on a train which was on top of yet another train going in another direction.

Some traditionalists did not care to take the train ride. Benny Goodman was not ready to be Elvinized, and Elvin's stay with Duke Ellington's band was brief. There is, however, an interesting 1962 record of Ellington playing piano with Coltrane and Elvin where on "Take the Coltrane",[75] Duke, for a moment, sounds like a modernist (in the style of Mal Waldron, or Sonny Clark) due to Elvin's influence. This strong, yet subtle, persuasion is heard on several other 1960's recordings when he was a sideman with Gil Evans's orchestra,[76] Stan Getz with Bob Brookmeyer,[77] Joe Henderson,[78] and McCoy Tyner,[79] among many others.

Elvin's sound is special. The small drums he used through the late '50s and '60s gave him his signature sound. His tuning is unique and identifiable.[80] In an interview with Arthur Taylor, Elvin mentions that his drum tuning is usually in fourths and fifths.[81]

---

[75] *Duke Ellington and John Coltrane* John Coltrane (9/26/62) Impulse CD MCAD-39103

[76] *Great Jazz Standards* Gil Evans (early 1959) Pacific Jazz CD CP32-5373 (Japan) Out of print in US
The Individualism of Gil Evans Gil Evans (7/9/64) Verve CD 833804-2

[77] *Bob Brookmeyer and Friends* Bob Brookmeyer (5/25/64) Columbia CD 468413 2 (Austria)

[78] *In and Out* Joe Henderson (4/10/64) Blue Note CD (Japan) CP32-5212

[79] *The Real McCoy* McCoy Tyner (4/2/67) Blue Note CD B21Y-46512

[80] See page 40 (THE INSTRUMENT)

[81] *Notes and Tones* Arthur Taylor (expanded edition) DaCappo

Elvin Jones abbreviated discography/timeline to 1970

1946-49   Army service *Swing, Not Spring—Savoy* CD SV-0188

1950-55   Plays with Detroit bands *Magnificent Thad Jones* ('57) BN LP1546

1955   Records with Miles Davis (7/9/55) *Blue Moods* OJCCD-043-2

1956   Moves to NY Art F. (11/23/56) *Farmer's Market* PR OJCCD-398-2

1956-57   Member of J.J. Johnson quintet *Live at Cafe Bohemia* FSRCD 143

1957   Records with Sonny Rollins at *Village Vanguard* (see p. 24, par. 2)

1957   Records with Pepper Adams *Savoy* (Japan) CDs SV-0161, SV-0198

1957-59   NYC jazz clubs *10 to 4 at the Five Spot—Riverside* OJCCD-031-2

1960-66   Member of John Coltrane quartet (see p. 22, par. 3)

1960   Records with Barry Harris *Preminado—Riverside* OJCCD-486-2

1961   Records first own album *Elvin—Riverside* RLP 409 and OJC 259

1964   Records with Wayne Shorter *Night Dreamer—Blue Note* B21Y84173

1964   Records with Wayne Shorter *JuJu—Blue Note* (Japan) CJ28-5105

1964   Records with Wayne Shorter *Speak No Evil—Blue Note* B21Y46509

1964   Records with Joe Henderson *Inner Urge—Blue Note* B21Y84189

1965   Records with Sonny Rollins *East Broadway Rundown—MCAD* 33120

1966   Begins leading a series of trios, quartets, sextets ('68) BN BST 84282

1972   Records quartet *Live at the Lighthouse—Blue Note* CDP7 84447, & 8

1978   Records first *Jazz Machine* album *Remembrance* (*MPS*)

1980-94   Continues to tour and record *The Jazz Machine*, lives in Japan

Quotes from Elvin

INTERNATIONAL MUSICIAN AND RECORDING WORLD, interviewer Zan Stewart

BRUSHES "I find brushes a fascinating part of the paraphernalia of rhythm, one of the rhythmic instruments I wish I could hear more. Shadow Wilson who used to be with Basie and Denzil Best, who was with Shearing, were the absolute masters of the art."

SOLO CONCEPT "A drum solo can be approached two ways, There's the abstract form of a solo that I sometimes utilize. Then there's the solo that's more idiomatic, that deals more with the composition. That's the same solo on drums that any other melodic instrument would play. I generally try to make it a combination of the two. Also, when I start a solo, I try to establish a rhythmic pattern on at least one level of the solo, so that is will serve as a metric point of reference, and from there, I try to make a varied interpretation of what the melodic line would be."

DOWNBEAT March 28, 1963, interviewer Don DeMicheal

RHYTHMS "Parker's approach demanded new drumming concepts and so does Coltrane's. In Parker's case the demand generally was for division of the time by two" (eighth and 16th notes, or duple meter); "Coltrane's present work most often gives rise to a feeling of three" (various forms of triplets, use of triple meters such as 3/4, 6/4, 6/8).

CONCEPT ORIGIN "It isn't something I developed deliberately. It's more or less a natural step, a natural thing to do. It was a step from staying away from the soloist, staying in the background, staying with the form of the composition without joining the soloist in his improvisation— the conventional way of playing."

PLAYING WITH (comping for) TRANE "It must be done with a great deal of discretion and feeling for what the soloist is doing. And I always realize I'm not the soloist, that John is, and I'm merely the support for him. It may sound like a duet or duel at times, but it's still a support I'm lending him, a complementary thing".

"It's being done in the same context of the earlier style, only this is just another step forward in the relationship between the rhythm section and the soloist. It's much freer—John realizes he has this close support, and, therefore, he can move further ahead; he can venture out as far as he wants without worrying about getting away from everybody and having the feeling he's out in the middle of a lake by himself."

SOUND BALANCE "Sound balance, that is the blending of sock cymbals, snare drum, bass drum, top cymbals, tom toms with the other instruments in the group. One thing can't be dominant over the other. For instance the bass drum can't be too loud or too consistent or your sock too sharp or heavy."

TEMPO "Sometimes I've used accelerandos and decelerandos in my solos. It seems a natural thing to do because it's a solo. And a solo can take any form the artist chooses; he can use any form he wants within the framework of the composition. It goes back to getting away from the rigidity that jazz had to face when it was primarily dance music."

RUDIMENTS/STICK CONTROL "I don't think rudiments, will ever be out of date. It's necessary to learn them for control, for developing your hands. But the emphasis shouldn't be placed only on them in instruction books. Rudiments are like scales, but you're not going to play scales on, say, a clarinet all your life. There's another step: the uses rudiments should be put to...to get into music. The control of the sticks is the most important thing to get; when you control the sticks, that's the first step toward controlling the instrument. You have to have the sticks under control before you can touch the instrument —and I mean touch, not beat on it. The drum is supposed to be played."

Down Beat Oct. 2,1969, interviewer Ira Gitler *"Playing the truth"* His brother Thad's tip—which has become Elvin's philosophy**:** *Thad Jones*—"Whenever you play, imagine that it's the very last chance or opportunity you'll ever have."

MELODY MAKER October 4, 1980, interviewer Walter Pass

REFLECTIONS OF COLTRANE YEARS "It has to be an awfully strong drive within your self to allow your spirit to emerge and mingle with others. And to know it's all right, and not be afraid of it. Those Coltrane years, that time went by without us even really being all that aware, because it just happened and it wasn't contrived"...."Now, people can use our experience vicariously. It is there. It has been done and accomplished, and one can look at that and say, okay—they did it."

"It's only when you have a group of people who are all very sensitive to that time-stream and who are plugged into it accurately, then is when you have the possibility for expansion. Then you can do all kinds of things because nobody is crippled by any shift in the time pattern. To listen effectively to a group like Coltrane's, you have to anchor onto something, one thing in that group that you can follow, and that will more or less allow you inside."

ON MAX He admires what Max Roach does for the solo drummer, but does not feel that he would be comfortable in that role. "I'm very happy to see Max do it because I don't think there's anybody who could do it better. Basically, his nature is that way, just as some Metropolitan Opera singer is a soloist. He is a virtuoso, and he is more effective as an artist in that context - for the instrument, for the whole scope of the art form."

PHILOSOPHY "New directions in drumming over the past decade? No. I haven't heard any at all. What's the point? There isn't any need for new directions. All those things that are here now were also around a 100 years ago. It's all there—it only has to be done."

MODERN DRUMMER 12/82, interviewer Rick Mattingly

ORIGINAL STYLE "No, I never questioned it. I knew I was doin the right thing. I also knew that it sounded complicated, but it was only an appearance of complication—it wasn't really. It wasn't status quo, so to speak, but I didn't feel that it was all that different. I grew up with the old methods and learned them, and then I had to reject them. Not really reject, but rather I chose to use the parts of them that suited me, which isn't exactly a rejection. I think it's an improvement. It adds more responsibility to the drummer, but it also offers greater opportunities.

"When approached properly, it broadens the musical scope of the player, and it has to be musical—it can't be an ego trip, something used to show off someone's personal achievement. It's not that kind of thing because it's not a gimmick. It's an addition to the responsibility that drummers have to eventually accept. One of the responsibilities involves being flexible enough to support the soloist within the full range of support. You won't be just following the soloist, but rather, you will become a partner".

THE INSTRUMENT: "It is one instrument, and I would hasten to say that I take that as the basis for my whole approach to the drums. It is a single musical instrument of several components".

"Playing in a small group context, I found that I didn't need the heavy timbre of, say, a 24" bass drum. It wasn't necessary. All I needed was something that would be felt throughout tat small group. And through a little experimentation, I found that by tightening the front head, making that taut, and making the beat head a little looser, I could control the pitch of the instrument without losing any of the tonal consistency".

"Basically, I've never really been a multi-drum man. I've always thought that even the snare drum has never been fully exploited. After all, you've got a tom-tom there as well. You can throw the snares off and there's a tom-tom. It's just a matter of having a throw-off that is efficient enough to expedite some sort of technique that would incorporate the snare strainer. And I think a snare drum and a tom-tom—the two together—is certainly sufficient for any kind of solo pattern. You could work up an endless variety of combinations with these two components. Add to that a bass drum, and perhaps a floor tom-tom, and that would be a handful in anybody's band."

...."You should certainly have what you need, although, it's another experience to be able to improvise the things that are not there. For instance, when playing the Latin-American style, you can improvise the sound of timbales or claves. This is some of the fun in playing drums— to be able to imitate those sounds. That's why it's such a wondrous instrument. It's an instrument with infinite variety, I think. So before acquiring all this superfluous material, I think it would be practical to explore the drumset from a simplistic point of view. One should reach a point of no-expansion, so to speak, before one expands.

Tony Williams

Anthony Williams   born Chicago, 12/12/45

Tony was two when his family moved to Boston where he grew up and studied with the great Alan Dawson. He was also influenced by Boston drummers William "Baggy" Grant and Jimmy Zitano. He played gigs with Boston jazz players when he was 15. He made his first major jazz record, "One Step Beyond" (3/1/62) with Jackie McLean for *Blue Note*. In May 1963 he joined the Miles Davis quintet and remained for six years until 1969. Herbie Hancock was the group's pianist. Bassists were Gary Peacock, and later Buster Williams, but Ron Carter was Davis's principal bassist. During that six year period with Miles, the rhythm section of Tony, Herbie, and Ron became unified. The classic combination was as important to the 1960s as Philly Joe Jones, Red Garland, and Paul Chambers had been earlier in the 1950s. They appeared on many important jazz recordings, including their own albums, through the 1960s. Saxophonist Wayne Shorter joined Davis in 1964 and remained until 1970. He became the "Coltrane component" of the Miles Davis 1960's quintet because of his originality and vitality.

After leaving Miles in 1969, Williams formed his first group, *Lifetime*, which featured organist Larry Young and guitarist John McLaughlin. Though not successful commercially, this exciting trio was innovative and pointed the way toward music of the early 1970s. Personnel changed, and after three years the group broke up. Later in the '70s Williams reunited with his Davis colleagues (and Freddie Hubbard replacing Miles) to perform and record with a group called *VSOP*. During the 1980s he appeared as a sideman on several jazz recordings, but didn't lead his own groups, on a regular basis, until later in the decade when he formed another quintet. His group, at this writing, includes saxophonist Bill Pierce, trumpeter Wallace Roney, and pianist Mulgrew Miller. They have played together for several years and record for *Blue Note*.

The following are some of Tony's innovations while with Miles Davis:

HI-HAT TECHNIQUES One of his inventions is a constant quarter note pulse played with the foot—similar to the traditional role of the bass drum. He uses a thick (marching band) cymbal as the bottom cymbal. This gives added definition to the foot stroke, and provides a more dominant role for the instrument. Like Elvin Jones, he phrases with his hi-hat in combination with other instruments of the set, especially the snare drum. A trademark is the linear cliché of four eighth notes—the first note played by the high-hat foot, closing on an upbeat—the next three notes played on the snare—"si -Ta-ta-ta".

BASS DRUM The high pitched sound of his 18 inch bass drum was similar to that of Jimmy Cobb, his predecessor with Miles. Since the drum sounded somewhat like a large floor tom-tom, Williams sometimes used it as such, integrating it with the other instruments—not just like an additional tom-tom a size larger, but more a hybrid between that sound and a bass drum—creating a virtually new sounding instrument.

RHYTHMIC MIXTURE By mixing rhythms, Williams achieves an illusion of changing tempo. Elvin Jones also uses this technique but in a less measured fashion. The effect to the listener is a tension and a temporary loss of the pulse. This deliberate disorientation is uniquely successful in changing our perspective of the music.

METRIC MODULATION An early example is in Wayne Shorter's "Footprints" (*Miles Smiles*) where Williams plays the theme mostly in meter of six and the improvisation in various related meters, often duple (double time swing 4/4 or Latin 2/4). These events have an effect similar to rhythmic mixture, but continue for longer intervals.

BROKEN TIME Williams effectively illustrates extreme examples of broken time in "Stella by Starlight" (*My Funny Valentine*) recorded at Philharmonic Hall. During the beginning, he stops playing altogether. He re-enters, then stops again. By weaving in and out of the music, using different rhythms (even eighth notes), styles (Bossa Nova), and techniques (rolling, etc.), he establishes an engaging dialogue.

Tony Willams abbreviated discography/timeline to 1970

1962 Jackie McLean *One Step Beyond* (out of print) *Blue Note* CD B21Y46821

1963 Miles Davis *Seven Steps to Heaven Columbia* CD CK-48827

1964 Records first album *Life Time* (out of print) *Blue Note* CD B21Y84180

1964 Miles Davis *My Funny Valentine, Four* (combination *Col.* CDs C2K-48821)

1964 Miles Davis *In Tokyo* (J) *Sony* 32DP 529, *In Berlin* (J) *Sony* CSCS 5147

1965 Records second *Blue Note* album *Spring* CD B21Y46135

1965 Miles Davis *ESP—Columbia* CD CK-46863

1966 Miles Davis *Miles Smiles—Columbia* CD CK-48849

1967 Miles Davis *Nefertiti—Columbia* CD CK-44113

1968 Miles Davis *Miles in the Sky—Columbia* CD CK-48954

1969 Miles Davis *In a Silent Way—Columbia* CD CK-40580

1969 Leaves Davis. His band *Lifetime* records *Emergency—Polydor*

Drummer Discography

Name Abrams, Lee   **Birth Date** 1/6/25

Birthplace New York, NY   **Reference** Grove / Feather (New)

Played with Roy Eldridge, Coleman Hawkins, J.J.Johnson, Oscar Pettiford, Wynton Kelly

Biography NYC. '50s played, recorded with pianists Eddie Heywood, Al Haig, Duke Jordan, Wynton Kelly; '52 - '53 played, recorded with Lester Young. Brother of saxophonist, Ray Abrams. Teacher in Brooklyn.

Album Title	Name of Artist	Label w Number	Date Recorded	Format	Country
First Sessions	Eddie Davis	Prestige PCD 24116-2	2/7/50	CD	US
Piano Interpretations	Wynton Kelly	Blue Note B21Y 84456	7/28/51	CD	US
Jordu	Duke Jordan	Vogue 655010	1/28/54	CD	FR
The Al HaigTrio	Al Haig	Fresh Sounds CD 038	3/13/54	CD	SP

Name Alexander, Mousey   **Birth Date** 6/29/22

Birthplace Gary, IN   **Reference** Grove / Feather (All)

Played with Benny Goodman, Zoot Sims, Al Cohn, Lee Konitz, Sonny Stitt, Clark Terry

Biography Elmer. NYC. '50s popular big band sideman, steady swing—Sauter-Finnegan Orchestra; '60s Sonny Stitt, Lee Konitz, Clark Terry—modern, mainstream styles; '70s/'80s moved to Florida. Own record *The Mouse Roars* FD LP 130.

Album Title	Name of Artist	Label w Number	Date Recorded	Format	Country
The Sound of S& F orchestra	Sauter-Finnegan	RCA LM 1009	1953	LP	US
Spirits	Lee Konitz	Milestone MSP-9038	3/1/71	LP	US
If I'm Lucky	Zoot Sims	Pablo OJCCD-683-2	10/27/77	CD	US
Warm Tenor	Zoot Sims	Pablo PACD 2310-831	9/18/78	CD	US

Name Ali, Rashied   **Birth Date** 7/1/35

Birthplace Philadelphia, PA   **Reference** Grove / Feather ('60s and '70s)

Played with Sonny Rollins, Paul Bley, John Coltrane, Sun Ra, Albert Ayler, Archie Shepp

Biography Robert Patterson. NYC. '65 - '67 John Coltrane; '68 - '69 Jackie McLean, Sonny Rollins, Archie Shepp; '70s concerts with other drummers; hosted new music club *Ali's Alley*, NYC. Strong free player. Own album: *Survival*. *Interstellar Space* is a duet album with John Coltrane.

Album Title	Name of Artist	Label w Number	Date Recorded	Format	Country
Meditations	John Coltrane	Impulse AS-9110	12/23/65	LP	US
Cosmic Music	John Coltrane	Impulse AS-9148	2/2/66	LP	US
Expression	John Coltrane	Impulse AS-9120	2/15/67	LP	US
Interstellar Space	John Coltrane	Impulse ASD-9277	2/22/67	LP	US

Name Altschul, Barry   **Birth Date** 1/6/43

Birthplace New York, NY   **Reference** Grove / Feather ('70s)

Played with Paul Bley, Chick Corea, Sam Rivers, Dave Holland, Anthony Braxton

Biography NYC. Late '60s Paul Bley, lived in Europe; '70s experimental stylist. '70- '72: formed the group *Circle* with Chick Corea, Dave Holland, and Anthony Braxton. Led own groups, own records *Muse, Sack*. Teacher and author.

Album Title	Name of Artist	Label w Number	Date Recorded	Format	Country
Closer	Paul Bley	ESP 1021	12/18/65	LP	US
Ramblin'	Paul Bley	Fontana 688608ZL	7/1/66	LP	US
Revenge	Paul Bley	Polydor 244046	6/2/69	LP	US
Songs of Singing	Chick Corea	Blue Note B21Y 90055	4/7/70	CD	US

Drummer Discography

Name Arnold, Horace E   **Birth Date** 9/25/37

Birthplace Wayland, KY   **Reference** Grove / Feather ('60s and '70s)

Played with Bud Powell, Charles Mingus, Chick Corea, Stan Getz, Roland Kirk

Biography aka Horacee. NYC. '60s artists listed. 1964 Bud Powell—his last Birdland performances. Leader of two of own recordings for CBS (listed); '80s teacher at William Patterson College.

Album Title	Name of Artist	Label w Number	Date Recorded	Format	Country
Is	Chick Corea	Solid State 18055	1969	LP	US
Tribe	Horacee Arnold	Columbia KC 32150	1973	LP	US
Tales of the Exonerated Flea	Horacee Arnold	Columbia KC 32869	1974	LP	US
Billy Harper quintet in Europe	Billy Harper	Soul Note 1001	1/24/79	CD	IT

Name Bailey, Colin   **Birth Date** 7/9/34

Birthplace Swindon, England   **Reference** Grove / Feather ('60s and '70s)

Played with Benny Goodman, Clare Fischer, George Shearing, Victor Feldman, Terry Gibbs

Biography LA. Early '60s came to US, settled in CA. Chet Baker, Victor Feldman, Joe Pass, studios; Dallas, TX 'late '70s - mid '80s Red Garland—then to Denver, CO. Large discography. Author: drum set books, including *Bass drum control*. Quick, light, versatile—fast bass drum—exciting soloist.

Album Title	Name of Artist	Label w Number	Date Recorded	Format	Country
*Catch Me	Joe Pass	Pacific Jazz TOCJ-5767	1963	CD	JA
*Joy Spring	Joe Pass	Blue Note LT 1103	2/6/64	LP	US
*For Django	Joe Pass	Pacific Jazz TOCJ-5309	10/64	CD	JA
*The Artful Dodger	Victor Feldman	Concord 4083	1/1/77	CD	US

Name Bailey, Dave   **Birth Date** 2/22/26

Birthplace Portsmouth, VA   **Reference** Grove / Feather (All)

Played with Gerry Mulligan, Lou Donaldson, Art Farmer, Kenny Dorham, Clark Terry, Charles Mingus

Biography NYC. '60s large, important discography Kenny Dorham, Gerry Mulligan. Swinging, consistent, steady accompaniment to both modern, and swing players. Administrator of NYC's Jazzmobile. Recorded own record dates including *Osmosis,* under different title/label.

Album Title	Name of Artist	Label w Number	Date Recorded	Format	Country
*Mainstream	Gerry Mulligan	EmArcy 826 993-2	9/21/55	CD	JA
*Hot Stuff from Brazil	Kenny Dorham	Westwind 2015	7/16/61	CD	GER
*T. Hayes and Clark Terry	Tubby Hayes	Columbia CK 45446	10/3/61	CD	US
*Osmosis	Kenny Dorham	Black Lion 760146	10/4/61	CD	GER

Name Bailey, Donald   **Birth Date** 3/26/34

Birthplace Philadelphia, PA   **Reference** Grove / Feather (All)

Played with Jimmy Smith, Hampton Hawes, Jimmy Rowles, Harold Land, Blue Mitchell

Biography aka Donald Duck. NY/LA. '50s—eight years with Jimmy Smith on East coast; mid-'60s—to LA Harold Land, Blue Mitchell, Hampton Hawes; '80s Carmen McRae,Sarah Vaughn. Light touch, swing, and ability to blend with singers and ensembles—popular accompanist.

Album Title	Name of Artist	Label w Number	Date Recorded	Format	Country
*The Sermon	Jimmy Smith	Blue Note CDP7 46097	8/25/57	CD	US
*Houseparty	Jimmy Smith	Blue Note CDP7 46546	8/25/57	CD	US
Here and Now	Hampton Hawes	Contemp.OJCCD-1782	5/12/65	CD	US
The Seance	Hampton Hawes	Contemp.OJCCD455-2	4/30/66	CD	US

Drummer Discography

Name Barth, Benny   **Birth Date** 2/16/29

Birthplace Indianapolis, IN   **Reference** Grove

Played with Mastersounds, Wes Montgomery

Biography SF. '50s Indianapolis, then to California Bay area where he remains active. Strong assertive bebop drummer.

Album Title	Name of Artist	Label w Number	Date Recorded	Format	Country
The Mastersounds	Mastersounds	Pacific Jazz M403	9/12/57	LP	US
Kismet	Mastersounds	World Pacific 243	4/22/58	LP	US
Mastersounds Live	Mastersounds	World Pacific 1269	4/11/59	LP	US
The Mastersounds	Mastersounds	Fantasy LP 3305	7/1/60	LP	US

Name Bateman, Edgar   **Birth Date**

Birthplace   **Reference**

Played with Walt Dickerson, Dave Burns, Ken McIntyre, Booker Ervin

Biography NYC. '50s Indianapolis; '60s NYC with artists listed. Swinging time. Interesting solos—original approach to motion (cross-sticking). Bop and avant-garde styles. Acknowledged by Bob Moses in *Drum Wisdom*.

Album Title	Name of Artist	Label w Number	Date Recorded	Format	Country
A Sense of Direction	Walt Dickerson	New Jazz OJCCD-1794	5/5/61	CD	US
Dave Burns	Dave Burns	Vanguard VRS9111	1962	LP	US
Way, Way Out	Ken McIntyre	United Artists 6336	1963	LP	US
The Trance	Booker Ervin	Fontana 88341	5/1/66	LP	DU

Name Bazley, Tony   **Birth Date** 9/10/36

Birthplace New Orleans, LA   **Reference** Feather ('60s)

Played with Wes Montgomery, Dexter Gordon, Harold Land, Teddy Edwards, Buddy Colette

Biography LA. Late '50s activie in LA jazz groups—swinging drummer.

Album Title	Name of Artist	Label w Number	Date Recorded	Format	Country
Leroy Walks	Leroy Vinnegar	Contemp.OJCCD160-2	7/15/57	CD	US
Carl Perkins Memorial	Carl Perkins	Fresh Sounds FSR099	10/2/57	CD	SP
Stax of Sax	Herb Geller	Fresh Sounds FSR 75	1958	CD	SP
Far Wes	Wes Montgomery	Pac.JazzCDP792596-2	4/1/58	CD	US

Name Bedford, Ronnie   **Birth Date** 6/2/31

Birthplace Bridgeport, CT   **Reference** Grove

Played with Buddy DeFranco, Rod Levitt, Benny Goodman, Chuck Wayne, Hank Jones

Biography NY. '60s - '70s Lee Konitz, Eddie Condon, Jack Reilly. Swinging, supportive accompanist. Currently lives and teaches in Wyoming.

Album Title	Name of Artist	Label w Number	Date Recorded	Format	Country
*Dynamic Sound Pattern	Rod Levitt	Riverside RM 471	7/1/63	LP	US
*RCA Jazz Workshop	Rod Levitt	RCA 6471-2-RB	2/10/64	CD	US
Arigato	Hank Jones	Progressive 7004	10/28/76	LP	JA
Over the Rainbow	Benny Carter	Music Masters 601964	10/18/88	CD	US

Drummer Discography

Name Bellson, Louis   **Birth Date** 7/26/24

Birthplace Rock Falls, IL   **Reference** Grove / Feather (All)

Played with Count Basie, Duke Ellington, Wardell Gray, Art Tatum, Zoot Sims, JATP

Biography NYC. '50s small groups with Wardell Gray *Capitol*, big bands—Ellington '51 - '53—innovative double bass drum use; '60s—own big band recordings *Verve*; '70s - '90s recordings own band, and sideman. Arranger/composer/educater/co-author:*4/4*, and *Odd Times Reading Texts*.

Album Title	Name of Artist	Label w Number	Date Recorded	Format	Country
Complete Ellington vols. 3,4	Duke Ellington	Columbia 462987 & 8	1951	2 CDs	AUS
*Ellington Uptown	Duke Ellington	Columbia CK40836	12/7/51	CD	US
*W. Gray and the Big Bands	Wardell Gray	Official 3029	2/1/52	LP	DU
*Zoot at ease	Zoot Sims	Famous Door HL-2000	5/30/73	LP	US

Name Berk, Dick   **Birth Date** 5/22/39

Birthplace San Francisco, CA   **Reference** Grove / Feather ('70s)

Played with Ted Curson, Don Friedman, Milt Jackson, Blue Mitchell, Cal Tjader

Biography NYC/LA. '60s NYC Walter Bishop, Don Friedman—then LA —George Duke, Cal Tjader. Strong swing—flexible accompanist. Own recordings: *Discovery* 877,890, and 922.

Album Title	Name of Artist	Label w Number	Date Recorded	Format	Country
*Flashback	Don Friedman	Riverside RLP 463	1963	LP	US
Bish Bash	Walter Bishop	Xanadu 114	8/2/64	LP	US
That's the Way it is	Milt Jackson	Impulse 9189	8/1/69	LP	US
Last Dance	Blue Mitchell	Jam 5002	4/28/77	LP	US

Name Best, Denzil   **Birth Date** 4/27/17   5/24/65

Birthplace New York, NY   **Reference** Grove / Feather (New)

Played with Ben Webster, Coleman Hawkins, Erroll Garner, George Shearing, Chubby Jackson, Fats Navarro

Biography NYC. DeCosta. '40s - '50s composer, pianist, bassist, and trumpeter. Brush master—one of the first to use smooth, circular, legato sweeps (Shearing *Savoy* CD SV-0208). Wrote "Bemsha Swing", "Wee", "Move". Bop innovators— Navarro, Konitz & swing greats—Webster, Hawkins.

Album Title	Name of Artist	Label w Number	Date Recorded	Format	Country
*Nostalgia	Fats Navarro	Savoy SV-0123	12/18/46	CD	JA
*Opus De Bop	Fats Navarro	Savoy SV-0118	1/29/47	CD	JA
*Be Bop Revisited	Chubby Jackson	Xanadu EPM FDC 5174	1/20/48	CD	FR
*Subconscious - Lee	Lee Konitz	Prestige OJCD-186-2	6/28/49	CD	US

Name Bishop, Wallace   **Birth Date** 2/17/06   5/1/86

Birthplace Chicago, IL   **Reference** Grove

Played with Jelly Roll Morton, Earl Hines, Buck Clayton, Sonny Stitt, Bud Powell

Biography NYC. '30s Earl Hines; '40s Billie Holiday, Louis Armstrong, and artists listed; 1951 moved to the Netherlands, where he stayed for the remainder of his life. Style somewhat similar to early Kenny Clarke—*Savoy* listings (only SV-0118 is currently available).

Album Title	Name of Artist	Label w Number	Date Recorded	Format	Country
*Opus De Bop	Sonny Stitt	Savoy SV-0118	8/23/46	CD	JA
*The Modern Jazz Piano	Bud Powell	Savoy ZD 70817	8/23/46	CD	US
*The Bebop Boys	Sonny Stitt	Savoy SJL 2225	8/23/46	2 LPs	US

Drummer Discography

Name Black, James

Birth Date

Birthplace New Orleans, LA

Reference

Played with Julian Adderley, Nat Adderley, Yusef Lateef

Biography New Orleans. Legendary modern jazz drummer. 12/82 interview *Modern Drummer.*

Album Title	Name of Artist	Label w Number	Date Recorded	Format	Country
*In the Bag	Nat Adderley	Jazzland OJCCD 648-2	6/1/62	CD	US
Live at Pep's lounge	Yusef Lateef	Impulse 9310	6/29/62	LP	US
Live at Pep's lounge	Yusef Lateef	Impulse 9353/2	6/26/64	LP	US
Live at Pep's lounge	Yusef Lateef	Impulse 9259	2/24/65	LP	US

Name Blackwell, Ed

Birth Date 10/10/29 10/7/92

Birthplace New Orleans, LA

Reference Grove / Feather ('70s)

Played with Ornette Coleman, Eric Dolphy, Booker Little, Don Cherry, Dewy Redman

Biography NYC. '60s Ornette Coleman, Eric Dolphy; '70s - '90s led own groups—*Old and New Dreams.* Important innovator/discography. Soloist— linear style, using traditional New Orleans drumming in modern (avant-garde) context. Also recommended: Lee Morgan *Fresh Sounds* FR CD1037.

Album Title	Name of Artist	Label w Number	Date Recorded	Format	Country
*Free Jazz	Ornette Coleman	Atlantic 1364-2	12/21/60	CD	US
*Ornette	Ornette Coleman	Atlantic SD 1378	1/31/61	LP	US
*Eric Dolphy at the Five Spot	Eric Dolphy	Prestige OJCCD-133-2	7/16/61	CD	US
*El Corazon (duets)	Don Cherry	ECM 829199-2	2/1/82	CD	GER

Name Blakey, Art

Birth Date 10/11/19 10/16/90

Birthplace Pittsburgh, PA

Reference Grove / Feather (All)

Played with Earl Hines, Billy Eckstine, Charlie Parker, Jazz Messengers

Biography NYC. See pages 37-39 for a more extensive biography. See page 21 for additional discography. These titles represent '50s sideman recordings. Recommended: *Sony* CD 25DP 5303 (Japan) *Jazz Messengers* (4/5/56), partially reissued in the US—Col. CD CK-47118.

Album Title	Name of Artist	Label w Number	Date Recorded	Format	Country
*The Brothers	Zoot Sims	Prestige OJCDD-008-2	9/8/52	CD	US
*H.S. and Jazz Messengers	Horace Silver	Blue Note B21Y 46140	11/13/54	CD	US
*The Unique Thelonious	Thelonious Monk	Riverside OJCCD-064-2	3/17/56	CD	US
*New Bottle, Old Wine	Gil Evans	Pacific Jazz CP32-5372	5/9/58	CD	JA

Name Bolden, Walter

Birth Date 12/17/25

Birthplace Hartford, CT

Reference Feather (New)

Played with Stan Getz, Howard McGhee, Horace Silver, Gigi Gryce, Lambert, Hendricks, and Ross

Biography NYC. '50s - '60s popular recording drummer—substantial modern discography Zoot Sims, Gerry Mulligan, Barry Harris, Allen Eager, Howard McGhee, Al Cohn. *Mulligan plays Mulligan* is a good example of extremely relaxed cool bop of the '50s.

Album Title	Name of Artist	Label w Number	Date Recorded	Format	Country
*Stan Getz Roost quartets	Stan Getz	Roulette B21Y 96052	12/10/50	CD	US
Mulligan plays Mulligan	Gerry Mulligan	Prestige OJCCD-003-2	9/21/51	CD	US
Cohn's Delights	Al Cohn	Vogue 655011	2/28/54	CD	FR
The Bebop Master	Howard McGhee	Affinity 765	10/22/55	CD	UK

Drummer Discography

Name Bradley, Will Jr.   **Birth Date** 2/15/38

Birthplace New York, NY   **Reference** Grove

Played with Woody Herman, Tony Scott, J. R. Monterose, George Wallington

Biography NYC. '50s Tony Fruscella, George Wallington, Bobby Scott, Jr. Monterose. Strong, swinging bop drummer—influenced by Arthur Taylor. Son of trombonist, Will Bradley.

Album Title	Name of Artist	Label w Number	Date Recorded	Format	Country
Tony Fruscella	Tony Fruscella	Atlantic P 7535A	3/29/55	LP	JA
*Jazz for Carriage Trade	George Wallington	Prestige OJCCD-1704	1/20/56	CD	US
In Celebration of Lester	Dave Pell	GNP S2122	1978	LP	US

Name Brice, Percy   **Birth Date** 3/25/23

Birthplace New York, NY   **Reference** Grove / Feather (New)

Played with Luis Russell, Benny Carter, Oscar Pettiford, Lucky Thompson, George Shearing, Ahmad Jamal

Biography NYC. '50s Billy Taylor, Kenny Burrell, Sarah Vaughn, George Shearing, Tiny Grimes; '60s Carmen McRae, Ahmad Jamal. Popular piano trio/group and vocal accompanist—nice brushes. Pettiford LP is part of 12 CD Charles Mingus box *Complete Debut recordings* 12CD-4402-2.

Album Title	Name of Artist	Label w Number	Date Recorded	Format	Country
Pendulum at Falcon's Lair	Oscar Pettiford	Debut OJC 112	12/29/53	LP / CD box	US
Cross Section	Billy Taylor	Prestige OJCCD-1730	7/30/54	CD	US
Billy Taylor with Candido	Billy Taylor	Prestige OJCCD-015-2	9/7/54	CD	US
Black Satin	George Shearing	Capitol C21S-92089	12/18/56	CD	US

Name Brooks, Roy   **Birth Date** 9/3/38

Birthplace Detroit, MI   **Reference** Grove / Feather ('70s)

Played with Horace Silver, Sonny Stitt, Dexter Gordon, Milt Jackson, Sonny Red, Charles Mingus

Biography NYC. '60s Horace Silver ('59-'64), Milt Jackson, Charles Mingus, large, important discography; '70s Max Roach's percussion ensemble *M'Boom*. Enthusiastic, swinging bop drummer.

Album Title	Name of Artist	Label w Number	Date Recorded	Format	Country
*Out of the Blue	Sonny Red	Blue Note TOCJ-4032	12/5/59	CD	JA
*Horace-scope	Horace Silver	Blue Note B21Y 84042	7/8/60	CD	US
*H. Silver at the Village Gate	Horace Silver	Blue Note B21Y 84076	5/19/61	CD	US
*Constellation	Sonny Stitt	Muse MCD 5323	6/27/71	CD	US

Name Brown, George   **Birth Date**

Birthplace   **Reference**

Played with Wes Montgomery, Sonny Stitt, Gene Ammons

Biography CHI/NYC. '50s recorded with Gene Ammons in Chicago; '60s several NYC recordings. Swings.

Album Title	Name of Artist	Label w Number	Date Recorded	Format	Country
Boss Tenors	Stitt and Ammons	Verve 837-440-2	8/1/61	CD	US
*Guitar on the Go	Wes Montgomery	Riverside OJCCD-489-2	10/10/63	CD	US
*Portrait of Wes	Wes Montgomery	Riverside OJCCD-144-2	10/10/63	CD	US

Drummer Discography

Name Brown, Phil   **Birth Date**

Birthplace   **Reference**

Played with Red Rodney, Stan Getz, Charlie Parker, Al Haig

Biography NYC. '50s recorded with important bop musicians. Getz's sound is badly distorted on *Birdland Sessions 1952* —however, the rest of ensemble is OK. Better sound on LPs: *Session* 108 and *Alto* 704. Exciting drum solo: "Move"—sounds like combination of Tiny Kahn and Buddy Rich.

Album Title	Name of Artist	Label w Number	Date Recorded	Format	Country
First Sessions	Red Rodney	Prestige 24116-2	9/16/50	CD	US
*Birdland Sessions 1952	Stan Getz	Fresh Sounds 149	8/9/52	CD	SWI
*CP. at Birdland/Cafe Society	Charlie Parker	Cool 'N Blue CD108	9/20/52	CD	SWI
Al Haig Quartet	Al Haig	Fresh Sounds 012	9/1/54	CD	SP

Name Bunker, Larry   **Birth Date** 11/4/28

Birthplace Long beach, CA   **Reference** Grove / Feather (All)

Played with Chet Baker, Gerry Mulligan, Art Pepper, Shorty Rogers, Bill Evans

Biography LA. '50s - '60s major voice, along with Manne, in the west coast movement. Hampton Hawes, Sonny Criss, Shorty Rogers, Art Pepper, one of Gerry Mulligan's first quartet drummers—brush master. Vibraphonist/pianist, popular Hollywood studio percussionist; '65 - '66 Bill Evans trio.

Album Title	Name of Artist	Label w Number	Date Recorded	Format	Country
*Surf Ride	Art Pepper	Savoy SV-0115	3/4/52	CD	JA
*Konitz meets Mulligan	Gerry Mulligan	Pacific JazzB21Y46847	1/1/53	CD	US
*Cool Baker vol.2	Chet Baker	PacificJazz6K18P9260	7/29/53	LP	JA
*Trio '65	Bill Evans	Verve POCJ-1908	2/3/65	CD	JA

Name Burroughs, Alvin   **Birth Date** 11/21/11   8/1/50

Birthplace Mobile, AL   **Reference** Grove

Played with Bill Harris, Earl Hines, Gene Ammons

Biography CHI. '40s transition drummer (swing to bop). Jo Jones credits him with using a coin in his hand to produce the first sizzle cymbal effect. This technique is heard on the Gene Ammons LP listed.

Album Title	Name of Artist	Label w Number	Date Recorded	Format	Country
*Small Herd on Keynote	Bill Harris	Mercury 830 968-2	4/5/45	CD	JA
*Jug Sessions	Gene Ammons	EmArcy 2-400	6/17/47	LP	US

Name Butler, Frank   **Birth Date** 2/18/28   7/24/84

Birthplace Kansas City, MO   **Reference** Grove / Feather (All)

Played with Art Pepper, Curtis Counce, Miles Davis, Harold Land, John Coltrane, Al Cohn

Biography LA. Late' 50s - mid '60s important discography. Influenced by Max Roach and Philly Joe Jones. '65 recorded *Kulu se Mama* with John Coltrane. Unaccompanied solo on *Sonority*. Own records. Original (so-called, California hard bop) style, somewhat similar to Higgins and Marable.

Album Title	Name of Artist	Label w Number	Date Recorded	Format	Country
*Sonority	Curtis Counce	Contemporary 7655-2	1/6/58	CD	US
*Seven Steps to Heaven	Miles Davis	Columbia CK- 48827	4/16/63	CD	US
The Stepper	Frank Butler	Xanadu 152	11/19/77	LP	US
Wheelin' and Dealin'	Frank Butler	Xanadu 169	10/22/78	LP	US

Drummer Discography

Name Campbell, Jimmy **Birth Date** 12/24/28
Birthplace Wilkes-Barre, PA **Reference** Feather (New)
Played with Woody Herman, Stan Kenton, Don Elliot, Hal McKusick, Tal Farlow
Biography NYC. '50s popular big band drummer with substantial discography (only small bands listed).

Album Title	Name of Artist	Label w Number	Date Recorded	Format	Country
Hal McKusick	Hal McKusick	Jubilee JLP 15	1955	LP	US
Urbie Green Septet	Urbie Green	Bethlehem BCP 14	1/19/55	LP	US
Sounds by Socolow	Frank Socolow	Bethlehem BCP 70	7/1/56	LP	US
This is Tal Farlow	Tal Farlow	Verve MGV 8289	6/1/58	LP	US

Name Campbell, Wilbur **Birth Date**
Birthplace **Reference**
Played with Charlie Parker, Gene Ammons, Ira Sullivan, Wilbur Ware, Kenny Dorham, Red Rodney
Biography CHI. '50s -'70s important modern drummer who played, recorded with many great players. Large discography. Original, loose style—somewhat similar to Elvin Jones, but more influenced by earlier drummers—Kenny Clarke, Philly Joe Jones, and Max Roach.

Album Title	Name of Artist	Label w Number	Date Recorded	Format	Country
*The Chicago Sound	Wilbur Ware	Riverside OJCCD-1737	11/18/57	CD	US
*Live at the Birdhouse	Ira Sullivan	Vee Jay NVJ2-950	3/12/62	2 CDs	US
The Chase	Gene Ammons	Prestige LP 10010	7/26/70	LP	US
*Charlie Parker Memorial	Kenny Dorham	Vogue 651600188	8/16/70	CD	FR

Name Capp, Frank **Birth Date** 8/20/31
Birthplace Worceter, MA **Reference** Grove / Feather (All)
Played with Stan Kenton, Terry Gibbs, Benny Goodman, Conte Candoli, Blue Mitchell
Biography LA. '50s - '90s popular big band, studio drummer with substantial discography.

Album Title	Name of Artist	Label w Number	Date Recorded	Format	Country
Jazz City Workshop	Herbie Harper	Bethlehem BCP 44	11/19/55	LP	US
The Mitchells	Blue Mitchell	Metrojazz E1012	10/6/58	LP	US
Candoli Brothers	Conte Candoli	Mercury MG 20515	1959	LP	US
Terry Gibbs Quintet	Terry Gibbs	Verve MGV 2136	3/10/60	LP	US

Name Carr, Bruno **Birth Date** 2/9/28
Birthplace New York, NY **Reference** Feather ('60s)
Played with Herbie Mann, Shirley Scott, Nat Adderley
Biography NYC. '60s Lou Donaldson, Abbey Lincoln, Ray Charles (*ABC Paramount*). Solid, steady time.

Album Title	Name of Artist	Label w Number	Date Recorded	Format	Country
Nat Adderley	Nat Adderely	Atlantic SD 1493	12/22/64	LP	US
Herbie Mann Today	Herbie Mann	Atlantic SD 1454	11/18/65	LP	US
Virgo Vibes	Roy Ayers	Atlantic SD 1488	3/6/67	LP	US
David Newman (title?)	David Newman	Atlantic SD 1524	12/2/68	LP	US

Drummer Discography

Name Carvin, Michael **Birth Date** 12/12/44

Birthplace Houston, TX **Reference** Grove / Feather ('70s)

Played with Freddie Hubbard, McCoy Tyner, Hampton Hawes, Dexter Gordon, Jackie McLean

Biography NYC. '70s drummer/percussionist with artists listed. Has led, recorded own groups.

Album Title	Name of Artist	Label w Number	Date Recorded	Format	Country
Live at Montmartre	Hampton Hawes	Arista AL 1020	9/2/71	LP	US
A Little Night Music	Dexter Gordon	Arista AF 1043	9/2/71	LP	US
New York Calling	Jackie McLean	SteepleChase 1023	10/30/74	CD	DEN
Antiquity	Jackie McLean/MC.	SteepleChase 1028	1974	CD	DEN

Name Catlett, Sidney **Birth Date** 1/17/10   3/25/51

Birthplace Evansville, IN **Reference** Grove / Feather (New)

Played with Louis Armstrong, Eddie Condon, Benny Goodman, Count Basie, Charlie Parker, Dizzy Gillespie

Biography aka Big Sid. NYC. Key '40s transition drummer. Favorite of Max Roach, Billie Holiday, and Louis Armstrong. Versatile in all jazz and dance band styles. Large, important discography. Recorded own bands. See *Drummin' Men* for bio. *Groovin* same as *Shaw*, better sound but no title "Shaw".

Album Title	Name of Artist	Label w Number	Date Recorded	Format	Country
*Complete Lester Young	Lester Young	Mercury 830 920-2	12/28/43	CD	JA
*Shaw 'Nuff	Dizzy Gillespie	Musicraft MVSCD-53	5/11/45	CD	US
*Groovin' High	Dizzy Gillespie	Savoy SV-0152	5/11/45	CD	JA
*Carnegie Hall concert	Hank Jones	Verve MGV 8132	4/5/47	LP	US

Name Ceroli, Nick **Birth Date** 12/22/39   8/11/85

Birthplace Warren, OH **Reference** Grove

Played with Stan Kenton, Warne Marsh, Milt Jackson

Biography LA. '70s with artists listed, author: Two part independence/co-ordination book for drummers.

Album Title	Name of Artist	Label w Number	Date Recorded	Format	Country
Ritchie	Ritchie Kamuca	Concord CJ 41	1977	LP	US
Warne Out	Warne Marsh	Interplay IP-7709	5/14/77	LP	US
Quietly There	Zoot Sims	Pablo OJCCD-787-2	3/20/84	CD	US

Name Chambers, Joe **Birth Date** 6/25/42

Birthplace Stoneacre, VA **Reference** Grove / Feather ('60s and '70s)

Played with Freddie Hubbard, Chick Corea, Bobby Hutcherson, Joe Henderson, *M'Boom*

Biography NYC. '60s - '90s large, important discography. Essence of late modern style. Strong, assertive swing combined with judicious accompaniment. Like Higgins, style is elegant, minimal, but attacks are broader, more aggressive. Pianist/percussionist/composer/leader—own recordings.

Album Title	Name of Artist	Label w Number	Date Recorded	Format	Country
*Dialogue	Bobby Hutcherson	Blue Note B21Y 46537	3/3/65	CD	US
*Mode for Joe	Joe Henderson	Blue Note B21Y 84227	1/27/66	CD	US
*Tender Moments	McCoy Tyner	Blue Note B21Y 84275	12/1/67	CD	US
*Figure and Spirit	Lee Konitz	Progressive 30CP-21	12/2/76	CD	JA

Drummer Discography

Name Charles, Dennis   **Birth Date** 12/4/33

Birthplace St. Croix   **Reference** Grove / Feather (New)

Played with Archie Shepp, Sonny Rollins, Cecil Tayor, Gil Evans, Steve Lacy

Biography NYC. Late '50s - '60s percussionist/drummer—original, flexible—active in avant-garde. *Jazz Advance* is recommended for his excellent early drumming, influenced by Art Blakey. '90s own groups, recorded *Queen Mary—Silkheart* SHCD-121.

Album Title	Name of Artist	Label w Number	Date Recorded	Format	Country
Jazz Advance	Cecil Taylor	Blue Note B21Y 84462	12/10/55	CD	US
*Soprano Sax	Steve Lacy	Prestige OJCCD-130-2	11/1/57	CD	US
*Great Jazz Standards	Gil Evans	Blue Note CP32-5373	2/5/59	CD	JA
Cell Walk for Celeste	Cecil Taylor	Candid 9034	1/9/61	CD	GER

Name Christensen, Jon   **Birth Date** 3/20/43

Birthplace Oslo, Norway   **Reference** Grove / Feather ('70s)

Played with Kenny Dorham, Stan Getz, Steve Kuhn, Dexter Gordon, Lee Konitz

Biography Europe. '60s Kenny Dorham, American bop musicians; '70s ECM recordings—known for "ECM sound"— a very clean, dry recording sound of his cymbals. Versatile in bop and '70s jazz styles.

Album Title	Name of Artist	Label w Number	Date Recorded	Format	Country
*Kenny Dorham	Kenny Dorham	RJD 515	1964	CD	FR
Alto Summit	Lee Konitz	MPS 15192	6/2/68	LP	GER
Afric Pepperbird	Jan Gabarek	ECM 1007	1970	LP	GER
Jon Christensen	Jon Christensen	Sonet SKA 1437	1976	LP	GER

Name Clark, Bill   **Birth Date** 7/31/25   7/30/86

Birthplace Jonesboro, AR   **Reference** Grove / Feather (New)

Played with Lester Young, Duke Ellington, Dizzy Gillespie, Mary Lou Williams

Biography NYC. '50s Lester Young, Dizzy Gillespie, George Shearing. Nice brushes.

Album Title	Name of Artist	Label w Number	Date Recorded	Format	Country
*Pres	Lester Young	Verve UMV 2672	7/1/50	LP	JA
*Lester Swings Again	Lester Young	Verve MGV-8181	7/1/50	LP	US
Dizzy Gillespie	Dizzy Gillespie	Atlantic LP 1257	3/25/52	LP	US
Arnold Ross Trio	Arnold Ross	Discovery DL 2006	4/1/52	LP	US

Name Clarke, Kenny   **Birth Date** 1/9/14   1/26/85

Birthplace Pittsburgh, PA   **Reference** Grove /Feather (All)

Played with Edgar Hayes, Louis Armstrong, Charlie Parker, Miles Davis, MJQ

Biography NYC. See pages 27-29 for a more extensive biography. Page 29 lists several excellent *Savoy* reissues. Examples here represent an overview of his giant discography. For more complete discography see *A Flower for Kenny* (Haggerty) or *Klook* (Hennessey)—see footnotes, p. 2.

Album Title	Name of Artist	Label w Number	Date Recorded	Format	Country
*Charlie Christian with Dizzy	Charlie Christian	Vogue 651 600135	5/12/41	CD	FR
*Miles Davis volume 1	Miles Davis	Blue Note B21Y 81501	5/9/52	CD	US
*Walkin'	Miles Davis	Prestige OJCCD -213-2	4/3/54	CD	US
*Ascenser Pour L' Echafaud	Miles Davis	Philips 83605-2	12/4/57	CD	GER

Drummer Discography

Name Clay, Omar   **Birth Date**

Birthplace   **Reference**

Played with Kenny Dorham, Gene Ammons, Frank Foster, Max Roach, Warren Smith

Biography NYC. '60s Kenny Dorham (drums '64); '70s - '90s drummer/percussionist—member of Max Roach's ensemble *M'Boom*. Most of discography is percussion—drums on Strata-East 7422.

Album Title	Name of Artist	Label w Number	Date Recorded	Format	Country
W.S. Composer's Workshop	Warren Smith	Strata-East SES 19723	1972	LP	US
*The Prime Element (perc.)	Elvin Jones	Blue Note LA-506 H2	7/24/73	2 LPs	US
We've Been Around (drums)	Warren Smith	Strata-East SES 7422	1974	LP	US
M'Boom Live at S.O.B.s (p)	M'Boom Max Roach	BlueMoon MRR279182	1/9/92	CD	US

Name Cobb, Jimmy   **Birth Date** 1/20/29

Birthplace Washington, DC   **Reference** Grove / Feather (All)

Played with Miles Davis, Cannonball Adderley, John Coltrane, Wynton Kelly, Hank Mobley

Biography Wilbur. NYC. '60s large, important discography. Influenced by Philly Joe Jones, following him in Miles Davis's quintet '58-'63. Strong, driving swing. Exciting, outstanding soloist—linear and cadential use of rudiments in solo phrases. All recordings with Davis are recommended.

Album Title	Name of Artist	Label w Number	Date Recorded	Format	Country
*Kind of Blue	Miles Davis	Columbia CK- 40579	3/2/59	CD	US
*Giant Steps	John Coltrane	Atlantic 1311-2	12/2/59	CD	US
*Carnegie Hall concert	Miles Davis	Sony 32DP 515	5/19/61	CD	JA
*Full House	Wes Montgomery	Riveride OJCCD-106-2	6/25/62	CD	US

Name Cobham, Billy   **Birth Date** 5/16/44

Birthplace Panama   **Reference** Grove / Feather (70s)

Played with Miles Davis, Horace Silver, *Mahavishnu Orchestra*, McCoy Tyner

Biography NYC. '70s powerful jazz/fusion player Miles Davis, *Mahavishnu Orchestra*—important in the development of '70s drumming styles. '80s - '90s leads his own successful groups.

Album Title	Name of Artist	Label w Number	Date Recorded	Format	Country
Big Fun	Miles Davis	Sony SRCS 5713-4	11/19/69	2 CDs	JA
*Live Evil	Miles Davis	Columbia CGT-30954	2/6/70	2 CDs	US
*Inner Mounting Flame	Mahavishnu Orch.	CBS CK- 31067	1971	CD	US
Fly with the Wind	McCoy Tyner	Milestone OJCCD-699	1/19/76	CD	US

Name Cocuzzo, Joe   **Birth Date** 9/17/37

Birthplace Boston, MA.   **Reference**

Played with Woody Herman, Gary McFarland, Erroll Garner, Don Ellis, *Immpropistional Jazz Workshop*

Biography NYC. '60s artists listed; '70s - '80s Tony Bennett; '90s active NYC accompanist—flexible, swinging style.

Album Title	Name of Artist	Label w Number	Date Recorded	Format	Country
The Music of Our Time	Leonard Bernstein	Columbia ML6133	1965	LP	US
*Profiles	Gary McFarland	Impulse A-9112	2/6/66	LP	US
Feeling is Believing	Erroll Garner	Mercury SR-61308	1970	LP	US
All of Me	John Pizzarelli	RCA Novus 631929	1990	LP	US

Drummer Discography

Name Cole, Cozy   **Birth Date** 10/17/06   1/29/81

Birthplace East Orange, NJ   **Reference** Grove / Feather (All)

Played with Louis Armstrong, Charlie Parker, Dizzy Gillespie, George Shearing

Biography NYC. William. Although his major contributions were in the '40s— swing period, like Rich he accompanied/recorded with important early modernists. Rudimental solos—"Bugle Call Rag" Armstrong (Decca MCA 82051)—are polyrhythmic.'50s first school for drummers with Krupa NY.

Album Title	Name of Artist	Label w Number	Date Recorded	Format	Country
*Blue Lester	Lester Young	Savoy SV- 0112	4/18/44	CD	JA
*Groovin' High	Dizzy Gillespie	Savoy SV- 0152	2/28/45	CD	JA
Great Britian's	George Shearing	Savoy SV- 0160	2/3/47	CD	JA

Name Collins, Rudy   **Birth Date** 7/24/34

Birthplace New York, NY   **Reference** Grove / Feather (All)

Played with Cootie Williams, Hot Lips Page, J.J.Johnson, Ray Bryant, Dizzy Gillespie

Biography NYC. '50s - '60s Woody Herman, Ray Bryant, Dizzy Gillespie, Kenny Burrell. Studied trombone before becoming drummer. Loose swing—popular, versatile accompanist—recorded with avant-garde pianist, Cecil Taylor (*United Artists*).

Album Title	Name of Artist	Label w Number	Date Recorded	Format	Country
Newport Jazz Festival	J.J. Johnson	Columbia CL 932	7/6/56	LP	US
Sounds of Africa	Ahmed Abdul-Malik	New Jazz 8082	8/22/62	LP	US
Bossa Nova Carnival	Dave Pike	New Jazz 8281	9/6/62	LP	US
*Dizzy G. and the Double Six	Dizzy Gillespie	Philips 830 224-2	9/20/63	CD	GER

Name Cooper, Jerome   **Birth Date** 12/14/46

Birthplace Chicago, IL   **Reference** Grove / Feather ('70s)

Played with Cecil Taylor, Lou Bennett, Steve Lacy, Sam Rivers

Biography NYC. '70s Active in avant-garde—Sam Rivers, Anthony Braxton, *Revolutionary Jazz Ensemble*, recorded several own albums.

Album Title	Name of Artist	Label w Number	Date Recorded	Format	Country
Revolutionary JazzEnsemble	R.J.E.	ESP 3007	11/1/71	CD	US
Manhattan Cycles	R.J.E.	India Navigation	12/31/72	LP	US
New York Fall 1974	Anthony Braxton	Arista AL 4032	9/27/74	LP	US

Name Copeland, Keith   **Birth Date**

Birthplace   **Reference**

Played with Billy Taylor, Johnny Griffin, Heath Brothers, Sam Jones, Charlie Rouse, Kenny Barron

Biography NYC. '70s Berklee teacher (Boston); late '70s—to NYC Billy Taylor; '80s - 90s popular small group accompanist, artists listed. Son of trumpeter, Ray Copeland. Own recording *On Target—Jazz Mania* JCD-6010.

Album Title	Name of Artist	Label w Number	Date Recorded	Format	Country
Return of the Griffin	Johnny Griffin	Galaxy 5117	10/17/78	LP	US
In Motion	Heath Brothers	Columbia JC35816	1/1/79	LP	US
The Bassist	Sam Jones	Interplay 7720	1/3/79	LP	US
Upper Manhat. Jazz Society	Charlie Rouse	Enja 4090-2	1/21/84	CD	GER

Drummer Discography

Name Cottler, Irv

Birth Date

Birthplace

Reference

Played with Barney Kessel, Jimmy Rowles, Frank Rosolino

Biography LA. '50s - '60s studios. Author: drum set chart reading book. Many years with Frank Sinatra.

Album Title	Name of Artist	Label w Number	Date Recorded	Format	Country
To Swing or Not to Swing	Barney Kessel	Contem.OJCCD-317-2	11/26/61	CD	US
Sessions LIve	Jimmy Rowles	Calliope 3023	6/26/55	CD	US
Frank Rosolino	Frank Rosolino	Reprise (9)6016	8/10/56	LP	US

Name Cyrille, Andrew

Birth Date 11/10/39

Birthplace New York, NY

Reference Grove / Feather ('70s)

Played with Cecil Taylor, Mary Lou Williams, Walt Dickerson, Roland Kirk, Jimmy Giuffre

Biography NYC. '60s - '90s Large discography: Marion Brown, Roland Kirk, Jimmy Giuffre, Grachan Moncur III. Versatile drummer—exciting soloist—original avant-garde stylist. Soloist/clinician. Own recordings.

Album Title	Name of Artist	Label w Number	Date Recorded	Format	Country
This is Walt Dickerson	Walt Dickerson	New Jazz OJCCD-1817	3/7/61	CD	US
Music of Ahmed Abdul-Malik	Ahmed Abdul-Malik	New Jazz 8266	5/23/61	LP	US
Nuba	Andrew Cyrille	Black Saint 0030	6/1/79	LP	IT
The Navigator	Andrew Cyrille	Soul Note 1062	9/21/82	LP	IT

Name Dawson, Alan

Birth Date 7/14/29

Birthplace Marietta, PA

Reference Grove / Feather (All)

Played with Lionel Hampton, Clifford Brown, Sonny Stitt, Jacki Byard, Booker Ervin, Dexter Gordon

Biography BOS. '50s-'90s Large, important discography. Teacher of many other great drummers: Tony Williams, Clifford Jarvis, Harvey Mason, Joe LaBarbera. Plays vibes. Berklee '57 - '75, Author: *A Manual for the Modern Drummer*. '70s D. Brubeck. Now active. Lives, teaches in Lexington, MA.

Album Title	Name of Artist	Label w Number	Date Recorded	Format	Country
*Cliff.Brown Big Band in Paris	Clifford Brown	Prestige OJCCD-359-2	9/28/53	CD	US
*The Blues Book	Booker Ervin	Prestige OJCCD-780-2	6/30/64	CD	US
*The Panther	Dexter Gordon	Prestige OJCCD-770-2	7/7/70	CD	US
*Tune Up	Sonny Stitt	Muse MCD- 5334	6/27/72	CD	US

Name Dean, Donald

Birth Date 6/21/37

Birthplace Kansas City, MO

Reference Grove / Feather ('60s)

Played with Kenny Dorham, Hampton Hawes, George Shearing, Phineas Newborn, Harold Land

Biography LA. '60s - '70s popular LA jazz drummer.

Album Title	Name of Artist	Label w Number	Date Recorded	Format	Country
Business Meetin'	Carmell Jones	Pacific Jazz LP53	1962	LP	US
Swiss Movement	Les McCann	Atalntic SD 1537	6/22/69	LP	US
Bluesmith	Jimmy Smith	Verve V6-8809	1/1/72	LP	US

Drummer Discography

Name DeJohnette, Jack   **Birth Date** 8/9/42

Birthplace Chicago, IL   **Reference** Grove / Feather ('70s)

Played with Jackie McLean, Charles Lloyd, Bill Evans, Joe Henderson, Miles Davis, Keith Jarrett

Biography NYC. '70s - '90s large, important discography. Miles Davis '69 - '72—recorded *Bitches Brew*—other dates. Own groups *Compost, Special Edition*. Composer—pianist—virtuoso jazz/fusion drummer. Co-authored (with Charlie Perry) *The Art of Modern Jazz Drumming* Hal Leonard.

Album Title	Name of Artist	Label w Number	Date Recorded	Format	Country
*Tetragon	Joe Henderson	Milestone MSP 9017	9/27/67	LP	US
*The Infinite Search	Miroslav Vitous	Warner Bros. P-7501A	11/1/69	LP	JA
*Miles Davis at the Fillmore	Miles Davis	Sony 50 DP 714	6/17/70	2 CDs	JA
*Standards vol.1	Keith Jarrett	ECM 811966-2	1987	CD	GER

Name Dennis, Kenny   **Birth Date** 5/27/30

Birthplace Philadelphia, PA   **Reference** Grove / Feather ('60s)

Played with Earl Bostic, Miles Davis, Thelonious Monk, Billy Taylor, Sonny Stitt

Biography NYC. Late '50s - early '60s recorded with artists listed—exciting style. Career slowed after 1965. Married singer, Nancy Wilson '63- 4. Unfairly compared to Philly Joe Jones and others.

Album Title	Name of Artist	Label w Number	Date Recorded	Format	Country
*The Congregation	Johnny Griffin	Blue Note1580	10/23/57	LP	JA
*Sonny Rollins/Thad Jones	Sonny Rollins	Zeta ZET 704	11/4/57	CD	FR
*Legrand Jazz	Michel Legrand	Philips 32 JD 159	6/25/58	CD	JA
Slide Hampton Octet (title?)	Slide Hampton	Strand SL 1006	1959	LP	US

Name Dentz, John   **Birth Date**

Birthplace   **Reference**

Played with Dave Schildkraut, Bill Triglia, Terry Gibbs, Joe Farrell, Chick Corea, Mose Allison,

Biography NYC/LA. '60s NYC—LA in late'60s/'70s; '70s - '90s popular, swinging LA accompanist—light, strong time. Somewhat reminiscent of Billy Higgins—*Darn that Dream*. Originally from NYC area.

Album Title	Name of Artist	Label w Number	Date Recorded	Format	Country
The Terry Gibbs quartet	Terry Gibbs	Limelight 82005	4/15/63	LP	US
Tempus Fugue it	Lou Levy	Interplay 7711	8/2/77	LP	US
Back to Birdland	Freddie Hubbard	Real Time 305	1980	CD	US
Darn that Dream	Art Pepper	Real Time RT 3009	3/23/82	CD	JA

Name DeRosa, Clem   **Birth Date**

Birthplace   **Reference**

Played with Charles Mingus, John LaPorta

Biography NYC. '50s active in experimental jazz groups.

Album Title	Name of Artist	Label w Number	Date Recorded	Format	Country
Jazz Experiments	Charles Mingus	Bethlehem BCP 65	12/1/54	LP	US
John La Porta	John LaPorta	Fantasy LP3-228	6/1/56	LP	US

Drummer Discography

Name Dixon, Ben   **Birth Date**

Birthplace   **Reference**

Played with Grant Green, Jack McDuff, John Patton, Dodo Marmarosa, Lou Donaldson

Biography NYC. '60s jazz/blues discography. Recorded with Marmarosa in Chicago.

Album Title	Name of Artist	Label w Number	Date Recorded	Format	Country
Ray Draper Quintet	Ray Draper	Prestige LP 7096	3/15/57	LP	US
Dodo Marmarosa	Dodo Marmarosa	Affinity 755	11/12/62	CD	UK
Natural Soul	Lou Donaldson	Blue Note LP 4125	5/9/62	LP	US
Grant's First Stand	Grant Green	Blue Note LP 4064	1/28/61	LP	US

Name Dodgion, Dottie   **Birth Date** 9/23/29

Birthplace Brea, CA   **Reference** Grove / Feather ('70s)

Played with Charles Mingus, Benny Goodman, Zoot Sims, Melba Liston, Marion McPartland

Biography NYC. '60s played with artists listed—solid, swinging drummer.

Album Title	Name of Artist	Label w Number	Date Recorded	Format	Country
Now 's the Time	Marion McPartland HAL115		1977	LP	US

Name Donald, Peter   **Birth Date** 5/15/45

Birthplace San Francisco, CA   **Reference** Grove

Played with Toshiko, Zoot Sims, John Abercrombie, Jimmy Mosher, Bill Perkins

Biography LA. Early '70s Boston—then LA studios, recordings. Bop, and contemporary '70s ECM styles—Abercrombie albums.

Album Title	Name of Artist	Label w Number	Date Recorded	Format	Country
Arcade	John Abercrombie	ECM-1-1133	1978	LP	GER
John Abercrombie Quartet	John Abercrombie	ECM-1-1164	1979	LP	GER
*A Chick from Chelsea	Jimmy Mosier	Discovery DS-860	5/1/81	LP	US
Journey to the East	Bill Perkins	Contemporary C-14011	11/19/84	LP	US

Name Donaldson, Bobby   **Birth Date** 11/29/22   7/2/71

Birthplace Boston, MA   **Reference** Grove / Feather (New and '70s)

Played with Count Basie, Benny Goodman, Sy Oliver, Andy Kirk, Lucky Millinder, Kenny Burrell

Biography NYC. '50s - '60s popular session drummer with large, varied discography—swing bands—small modern groups. Composer.

Album Title	Name of Artist	Label w Number	Date Recorded	Format	Country
Essais	Andre Hodier	Savoy SJL 1194	3/5/57	LP	US
Flute Souffle	Herbie Mann	Prestige OJCCD-760-2	3/12/57	CD	US
Guitar Soul	Kenny Burrell	Prestige LP 7448	5/10/57	LP	US
Images	Curtis Fuller	Savoy SV-0129	6/7/60	CD	JA

Drummer Discography

Name Dowdy, Bill   **Birth Date** 8/15/33

Birthplace Benton Harbor, MI   **Reference** Grove / Feather (New and '60s)

Played with Nat Adderley, Three Sounds, Lou Donaldson

Biography NYC.Late '50s - early '60s *Three Sounds*—strong swing.

Album Title	Name of Artist	Label w Number	Date Recorded	Format	Country
Branching Out	Nat Adderley	RiversideOJCCD-255-2	1958	CD	US
Introducing The 3 Sounds	The Three Sounds	Blue Note B21Y 46531	9/16/58	CD	US
L. D. with the Three Sounds	Lou Donaldson	Blue Note BLP 4012	2/12/59	LP	US

Name Dreares, Al   **Birth Date** 1/4/29

Birthplace Key West, FL   **Reference** Grove / Feather (New)

Played with Charles Mingus, Kenny Burrell, Phineas Newborn, Teddy Charles, Freddie Redd

Biography NYC. '50s Gigi Gryce, Benny Green, Freddie Redd; percussion teacher;1985—moved to Miami.

Album Title	Name of Artist	Label w Number	Date Recorded	Format	Country
Jazz Ala Bohemia	Randy Weston	Riverside OJCCD-1747	10/25/56	CD	US
San Francisco Suite	Freddie Redd	Riverside OJCCD-1748	10/2/57	CD	US
Walkin' and Talkin'	Benny Green	Blue Note TOCJ-4010	1/25/59	CD	JA
* Benny Green	Benny Green	Bainbridge 1046	9/27/60	CD	US

Name Drootin, Buzzy   **Birth Date** 4/22/10

Birthplace Russia   **Reference** Grove / Feather (All)

Played with Boyd Raeburn, Serge Chaloff, Dizzy Gillespie

Biography NYC/BOS. '40s -' 50s Boston early modernists. Large traditional discography (Eddie Condon and others).

Album Title	Name of Artist	Label w Number	Date Recorded	Format	Country
*Serge & Boots (Fable of M.)	Serge Chaloff	Storyville 32 JDS-165	6/9/54	CD	JA
D.Gillespie and Bob. Hackett	Dizzy Gillespie	Europa Jazz EJ-1024	1960	LP	IT

Name Dukes, Joe   **Birth Date**

Birthplace   **Reference**

Played with Kenny Burrell, Gene Ammons, Lonnie Smith, Jack McDuff

Biography NYC. '60s solid swing—substantial discography: organ/blues groups—own *Prestige* album.

Album Title	Name of Artist	Label w Number	Date Recorded	Format	Country
Soul Summit	Gene Ammons	Prestige 24118-2	1/23/62	CD	US
J. McDuff feat. Kenny Burrell	Jack McDuff	PrestigePRCD24131-2	2/26/63	CD	US
The Soulful Drums	Joe Dukes	PrestigePRLP 7324	5/14/64	LP	US
Drives	Lonnie Smith	Blue Note CDP7 72432	2/2/70	CD	US

Drummer Discography

Name Dunlop, Frank			**Birth Date** 12/6/28		
Birthplace Buffalo, NY			**Reference** Grove / Feather (All)		

Played with Thelonious Monk, Charles Mingus, Sonny Rollins

Biography NYC. Late '50s - '60s Maynard Ferguson, Duke Ellington, Lionel Hampton. Recordings and tours with T. Monk—3 years (early '60s). Strong, swinging time. Interesting solos—simple linear phrases—modern/swing influence. There have been rumors of his ill health, and death in '80s.

Album Title	Name of Artist	Label w Number	Date Recorded	Format	Country
*Criss Cross	Thelonious Monk	Sony Columbia 469184	2/26/63	CD	AUS
*Always Know	Thelonious Monk	Sony Columb.4691852	7/4/63	2 CDs	AUS
* Monk Big Band and Quartet	TheloniousMonk	Sony Columbia 468408	12/30/63	CD	AUS
* Alfie	Sonny Rollins	Impulse MCA 39017	1/26/66	CD	US

Name Durham, Bobby			**Birth Date**		
Birthplace			**Reference**		

Played with Tommy Flanagan, Monty Alexander, Sonny Stitt, Dizzy Gillespie, JATP

Biography NYC. '70s substantial discography, includes many sessions for Norman Granz— *Pablo*.

Album Title	Name of Artist	Label w Number	Date Recorded	Format	Country
Tokyo Festival	Tommy Flanagan	Pablo 2310-724	2/15/75	LP	US
Montreux 77	Tommy Flanagan	Pablo 2308-202	7/13/77	LP	US
Back To My Own Home Town	Sonny Stitt	Black & Blue 59.724	11/12/79	CD	FR
Alternate Blues	Dizzy Gillespie	Pablo 2312-136	3/10/80	LP	US

Name Edghill, Arthur			**Birth Date** 7/21/26		
Birthplace New York, NY			**Reference** Grove / Feather (New)		

Played with Gigi Gryce, Horace Silver, Shirley Scott, Kenny Dorham, Mal Waldron, Dinah Washington

Biography NYC. '50s with artists listed. Kenny Dorham's *Jazz Prophets*.

Album Title	Name of Artist	Label w Number	Date Recorded	Format	Country
The Jazz Prophets	Kenny Dorham	MCA VIM 5575M	4/4/56	LP	JA
At Cafe Bohemia vol. 1	Kenny Dorham	Blue Note B21Y 46541	5/31/56	CD	US
At Cafe Bohemia vol. 2	Kenny Dorham	Blue Note B21Y 46542	5/31/56	CD	US
Mal-1	Mal Waldron	Prestige OJCCD -611-2	11/8/56	CD	US

Name Elgart, Billy			**Birth Date**		
Birthplace			**Reference**		

Played with Sam Rivers, Randy Weston, Keith Jarrett, Paul Bley, Mick Goodrick, Kenny Wheeler

Biography NYC/Europe. '60s Boston Sam Rivers, Keith Jarrett— NYC Randy Weston; '70s - 90s Germany. Very interesting, original avant-garde drummer. Discography slowed until '90s— recent Italian recordings, listed.

Album Title	Name of Artist	Label w Number	Date Recorded	Format	Country
*Paul Bley with Gary Peacock	Paul Bley	ECM 1003	5/10/68	LP	GER
* Mr. Joy	Paul Bley	Limelight LS86060	5/11/68	LP	US
Cities	Claudio Fasoli	Ram RM CD4503	1993	CD	IT
Tales	P. Dalla Porta	Soul Note 121244-2	1993	CD	IT

Drummer Discography

Name Ellington, Steve   **Birth Date**

Birthplace   **Reference**

Played with   Hal Galper, Sam Rivers, Roland Kirk, Hampton Hawes, Art Farmer, Dave Holland

Biography   LA/NYC. '60s Boston: Sam Rivers, Hal Galper— then NYC: Roland Kirk—then California: Hampton Hawes; '90s; Hal Galper, Dave Holland. Original, swinging drummer— interesting discography.

Album Title	Name of Artist	Label w Number	Date Recorded	Format	Country
Green Leavesof Summer	Hampton Hawes	Contem. OJCCD-476-2	2/17/64	CD	US
A New Conception	Sam Rivers	Blue Note 4249	10/11/66	LP	US
On the Road	Art Farmer	Contem.OJCCD-478-2	7/26/76	CD	US
Invitation to a Concert	Hal Galper	Concord CCD-4455	1990	CD	US

Name English, Bill   **Birth Date** 8/27/25

Birthplace New York, NY   **Reference** Grove

Played with   Bennie Green, Gene Ammons, Kenny Burrell, Quincy Jones, Joe Newman

Biography   NYC. Mid '50s - '60s popular mainstream jazz/blues drummer. Own *Vanguard* recording.

Album Title	Name of Artist	Label w Number	Date Recorded	Format	Country
Walking Down	Benny Green	Prestige OJCCD -1752	6/26/56	CD	US
Bill English	Bill English	Vanguard LP 9127	1963	LP	US
Gene Ammons	Gene Ammons	Prestige LP 7275	6/13/61	LP	US
Midnight Blue	Kenny Burrell	Blue Note B21Y 46399	1/7/63	CD	US

Name Evans, Sticks   **Birth Date**

Birthplace   **Reference**

Played with   Gunther Schuller, Charles Mingus, John Lewis, Eric Dolphy

Biography   NYC. '60s percussionist/tympanist/drummer—several recording dates with Gunther Schuller.

Album Title	Name of Artist	Label w Number	Date Recorded	Format	Country
Kai Winding	Kai Winding	Impulse A(S) 3	12/13/60	LP	US
*Jazz Abstractions	John Lewis	Atlantic AMCY 1093	12/19/60	CD	JA
*Vintage Dolphy	Eric Dolphy	GM 3005 CD	3/14/63	CD	US

Name Fields, Kansas   **Birth Date** 12/5/15

Birthplace Chapman, KS   **Reference** Grove / Feather (New)

Played with   Bud Powell, Benny Goodman, Sidney Bechet, Dizzy Gillespie

Biography   Carl Donnell. NYC/ Europe. Late '40s - early '50s NYC; 1953 moved to Europe—stayed. Versatile, popular drummer. Swinging time. Played and recorded with many jazz greats, including early modernists— Clyde Hart, Bud Powell and Dizzy Gillespie.

Album Title	Name of Artist	Label w Number	Date Recorded	Format	Country
School Days	Dizzy Gillespie	Savoy SV-0157	3/1/51	CD	JA
*The Champ	Dizzy Gillespie	Savoy SV-0170	3/1/51	CD	JA
*Bud Powell in Paris	Bud Powell	Discovery DS830	2/1/63	CD	US
Dizzy Gillespie	Dizzy Gillespie	Limelight LM82007	11/4/64	LP	US

Drummer Discography

Name Finch, Otis   **Birth Date** 1933   7/13/82

Birthplace   **Reference** Grove

Played with Dizzy Gillespie, Milt Jackson , Gene Ammons

Biography aka Candy. NYC. '60s popular recording drummer—small jazz /blues groups—loose swing.

Album Title	Name of Artist	Label w Number	Date Recorded	Format	Country
Shirley S. plays Horace Silver	Shirley Scott	Prestige PRLP 7240	11/17/61	LP	US
Dave Burns	Dave Burns	VanguardVRS9143	1/1/64	LP	US
Let 'em Roll	John Patton	Blue Note B21Y 89795	12/11/65	CD	US
Born Free	Milt Jackson	Limelight LM82045	1967	LP/CD	US/JA

Name Flores, Chuck   **Birth Date** 1/5/35

Birthplace Orange, CA   **Reference** Grove / Feather (New)

Played with Woody Herman, Art Pepper, Shorty Rogers, Bud Shank, Conte Candoli

Biography LA. '50s Woody Herman, Art Pepper; '60s popular recording artist; teacher. Solid, swinging time. Recorded with Woody Herman's big band for *Capitol*. The recorded sound of his cymbals is distorted on *The Art of Pepper*. *Modern Art* has better recorded sound.

Album Title	Name of Artist	Label w Number	Date Recorded	Format	Country
Modern Art	Art Pepper	Blue Note CDP746848	4/1/57	CD	US
*West Coast Jazz	Art Pepper	Zeta 729	3/31/57	CD	FR
*The Art of Pepper	Art Pepper	Blue Note CDP746853	4/1/57	CD	US
Mucho Calor	Art Pepper	VSOP #47 CD	4/24/58	CD	US

Name Foster, Al   **Birth Date** 1/18/44

Birthplace Richmond,VA   **Reference** Grove

Played with Miles Davis, Joe Henderson, Steve Kuhn, Sonny Rollins, Art Pepper, Tommy Flanagan

Biography NYC. Late '60s Earl May, Larry Willis; '70s - '90s very popular sideman with large, important discography. '80s Miles Davis—effective combination of jazz/rock style (The two Miles Davis titles listed), although he is basically a jazz drummer—versatile, solid, swinging accompanist.

Album Title	Name of Artist	Label w Number	Date Recorded	Format	Country
*D. Jordan with Cecil Payne	Duke Jordan	Xanadu 151792	3/16/73	CD	FR
*We Want Miles	Miles Davis	Sony CSCS 5131	10/4/81	2 CDs	JA
*Miles! Miles! Miles!	Miles Davis	Sony SRCS 6513-4	10/4/81	2 CDs	JA
*Life's Magic	Steve Kuhn	Black Hawk 522-2	3/28/86	CD	US

Name Fournier, Vernel   **Birth Date** 7/30/28

Birthplace New Orleans, LA   **Reference** Grove / Feather (New and '60s)

Played with George Shearing, Ahmad Jamal, Norman Simmons, Clifford Jordan

Biography CHI/NYC. Late '50s Ahmad Jamal—brush master—relaxed, but solid time. '60s - '90s active in NYC. Great drummer— consistently. Some of Jamal's LPs have been reissued on *Chess* CD *At the Pershing* CHS-9109. MHS CD available from *The Musical Heritage Society* (Ocean, NJ).

Album Title	Name of Artist	Label w Number	Date Recorded	Format	Country
*But Not for Me	Ahmad Jamal	Argo LP 628	1/16/58	LP	US
*At the Pershing vol. 2	Ahmad Jamal	Argo LP 667	1/17/58	LP	US
*Down Through the Years	Clifford Jordan	Milestone 9197	1987	CD	US
*Live at Ethell's	Clifford Jordan	MHS 512629A	10/16/87	CD	US

Name Free, Ronnie   **Birth Date** 1/15/36

Birthplace Charleston, SC   **Reference** Feather (New)

Played with Mose Allison, George Wallington, Lennie Tristano, LeeKonitz

Biography NYC. Active in the late '50s - early '60s.

Album Title	Name of Artist	Label w Number	Date Recorded	Format	Country
Ramblin' with Mose	Mose Allison	Prestige PR 7215	4/18/58	LP	US
Creek Bank	Mose Allison	PrestigeOJCCD-24055	8/15/58	CD	US
Greatest Hits	Mose Allison	PrestigeOJCCD-6004	2/13/59	CD	US
L. Konitz meets Jim. Guiffrie	Lee Konitz	Verve 23 MJ 3172	5/12/59	CD	JA

Name Freeman, Bruz   **Birth Date**

Birthplace Chicago, IL   **Reference**

Played with Charlie Parker, Hampton Hawes, Jim Hall, Lorraine Geller

Biography CHI/LA. Early '50s Chicago with brother,Von Freeman, Bird—then to LA ('50s).

Album Title	Name of Artist	Label w Number	Date Recorded	Format	Country
An Evening at Home	Charlie Parker	Savoy SV- 0154	10/1/50	CD	JA
Lorraine Geller	Lorraine Geller	Fresh Sounds 195	1954	CD	SWI
All Night Session vol. 1	Hampton Hawes	Contem. OJCCD-638-2	11/12/56	CD	US
All Night Sessions vols.2&3	Hampton Hawes	Con.OJCCDs 639 & 40	11/12/56	2 CDs	US

Name Frommer, Gary   **Birth Date**

Birthplace   **Reference**

Played with Art Pepper, Jack Sheldon

Biography CHI/LA. '50s recorded in Chicago—then west coast—Pepper and others.

Album Title	Name of Artist	Label w Number	Date Recorded	Format	Country
Val's Pal	Art Pepper	Tampa TP 20	8/1/56	LP	US
The Way it Was	Art Pepper	Contem. OJCCD-389-2	11/26/56	CD	US

Name Gant, Frank   **Birth Date**

Birthplace   **Reference**

Played with Sonny Stitt, J. J. Johnson, Ahmad Jamal, Donald Byrd, Ahmad Jamal, Barry Harris, Al Haig

Biography DET/NYC. '50s Detroit: Yusef Lateef, Barry Harris—then NYC in '60s; J.J.Johnson and artists listed; '70s - '80s with artists listed. Original, light, swinging bop style, influenced by Max Roach and Philly Joe Jones. Substantial, important discography.

Album Title	Name of Artist	Label w Number	Date Recorded	Format	Country
First Flight	Donald Byrd	Delmark DD-407	8/23/55	CD	US
*Breakin' it up	Barry Harris	Cadet 644 (Baybridge)	7/31/58	LP	US/JA
*Burnin'	Sonny Stitt	Argo 661	8/1/58	LP	US/JA
Proof Positive	J. J. Johnson	Impulse (S) 68	5/1/64	LP	US

Drummer Discography

Name Gladden, Eddie

Birth Date 12/6/37

Birthplace NJ

Reference Grove / Feather ('70s)

Played with Dexter Gordon, Horace Silver, Shirley Scott, Kenny Dorham, Cecil Payne, Larry Young

Biography NY. '60s - '70s drummer with one of the first Dexter Gordon quartets, after Dexter's return to US. in late '70s. Strong, steady swinging time—exciting solos. Substantial discography with important players.

Album Title	Name of Artist	Label w Number	Date Recorded	Format	Country
Sojourn	Mickey Tucker	Xanadu 143	3/28/77	LP	US
Manhattan Symphonie	Dexter Gordon	Sony 25 DP 5326	5/2/78	CD	JA
*Nights at the Keystone vol.1	Dexter Gordon	Blue Note CDP 794848	5/13/78	CD	US
Great Encounters/D. Gordon	Dexter Gordon	Columbia JC-35978	5/1/78	LP	US

Name Goodwin, Bill

Birth Date 1/8/42

Birthplace LA , CA

Reference Grove / Feather ('60s and '70s)

Played with Art Pepper, Gerry Mulligan, Gary Burton, Chuck Israels, Phil Woods

Biography LA/NYC. Late '60s LA—then to NYC '70s—strong assertive accompanist/solist. '80s -'90s Phil Woods' drummer for many years. Producer. Own recording: *Three is a Crowd* TCB CD 93402

Album Title	Name of Artist	Label w Number	Date Recorded	Format	Country
I've been doin' some thinking	Mose Allison	Atlantic SD 1511	7/9/68	LP	US
*Gary B and Keith Jarrett	Gary Burton	Atlan. (Rhino) R271594	7/23/70	CD	US
*National Jazz Ensemble	Chuck Israels	Churiasco 140 and152	5/1/75	3 LPs	US
The P.W. Quartet 'More' Live	Phil Woods	Mobile Fidelity 775	5/23/78	CD	US

Name Granelli, Jerry

Birth Date 12/30/40

Birthplace San Francisco, CA

Reference Grove / Feather ('60s)

Played with Vince Guaraldi, Denny Zeitlin, John Handy, Mose Allison

Biography SF. '60s Denny Zeitlin; '70's - '90s acoustic jazz groups—interesting, original jazz drummer. Own recordings; *One Day at a Time* ITM CD 970055; *I Thought I Heard Buddy Sing* ECD 22057.

Album Title	Name of Artist	Label w Number	Date Recorded	Format	Country
The Latin Side of V.Guaraldi	Vince Guaraldi	Fantasy 3360	1964	LP	US
Carnival	Denny Zeitlin	Columbia CS9140	1994	LP	US
Zeitgeist	Denny Zeitlin	Columbia CS9548	1966	LP	US
Your Mind is on Vacation	Mose Allison	Atlantic SD 1691	4/5/76	LP	US

Name Granowsky, Harold

Birth Date

Birthplace

Reference

Played with Lennie Tristano, Joe Roland, Phil Sunkel

Biography aka Hal Grant. NYC. Late '40s with artists listed—recorded legendary *Capitol* Tristano sessions.

Album Title	Name of Artist	Label w Number	Date Recorded	Format	Country
*Jazz into Cool	Lennie Tristano	Capitol TOCJ-5700	3/4/49	CD	JA
Joltin' Joe	Joe Roland	Savoy MG15034	1/27/50	LP	US
Phil Sunkel	Phil Sunkel	ABC 136	1956	LP	US
Lenny Hambro	Lenny Hambro	Epic LN 3361	5/9/56	LP	US

Drummer Discography

Name Graves, Milford   **Birth Date** 8/20/41

Birthplace New York, NY   **Reference** Grove / Feather ('60s and '70s)

Played with Albert Ayler, Don Pullen, NY Art Quartet, Roswell Rudd, Lowell Davidson

Biography NYC. Mid to late '60s active in avant-garde—original style; '70s—1973 Bennington College teacher. Continues to perform. Has recorded own sessions and duets with Andrew Cyrille. Very exciting, busy free player —*ESP* dates.

Album Title	Name of Artist	Label w Number	Date Recorded	Format	Country
Barrage	Paul Bley	ESP 1008	10/20/64	CD	US
NY Art Quartet	Roswell Rudd	ESP 1004	7/27/65	CD	US
Love Cry	Albert Ayler	Impulse GRD-108	8/31/67	CD	US
*Lowell Davidson Trio	Lowell Davidson	ESP 1012	11/1/69	CD	US

Name Gubin, Sol   **Birth Date** 7/11/28

Birthplace Atlantic City, NJ   **Reference**

Played with Elliot Lawrence, Benny Goodman, Count Basie, Stan Kenton, Zoot Sims, Al Cohn

Biography NYC/LA. '50s - '60s NYC studios, outstanding big band records: Elliot Lawrence *Steel Pier*, Stan Kenton *Cuban Fire* (perc), Bill Potts *Bye Bye Birdie*, Leonard Bernstein *Prelude, Fugues & Riffs*; '70s -90s LA—recently with Frank Sinatra. Important, swinging big band drummer.

Album Title	Name of Artist	Label w Number	Date Recorded	Format	Country
*E.L.plays argmts. Tiny Kahn	Elliot Lawrence	Fantasy ?	1950s	LP	US
*Big Band Sound	Elliot Lawrence	Fresh Sounds 2003	5/26/58	CD	SWI
*Legrand Jazz	Michel LeGrand	Philips 32 JD 159	12/6/62	CD	JA
Swinging Friends	Gene Roland	Brunswick BL54114	5/22/63	LP	US

Name Guerin, John   **Birth Date** 10/31/39

Birthplace Hawaii   **Reference** Grove / Feather ('70s)

Played with Buddy DeFranco, George Shearing, Oliver Nelson, Thelonious Monk, Ray Brown, Milt Jackson

Biography LA. Mid '60s - '80s Vic Feldman, Tom Scott, studios; '90s (late '80s) movie soundtrack *Bird*. Swinging LA studio drummer.

Album Title	Name of Artist	Label w Number	Date Recorded	Format	Country
Mike Wofford	Mike Wofford	Epic LN 26225	1966	LP	US
*Monk's Blues	Thelonious Monk	ColumbiaCBS4671822	12/19/68	CD	AUS
Brown's Bag	Ray Brown	Concord CJ 19	12/1/75	LP	US
Big Mouth	Milt Jackson	Pablo 2310.867	2/26/81	LP	US

Name Hadden, Skip   **Birth Date** 8/24/45

Birthplace Port Chester, NY   **Reference**

Played with Bill DeArango, Ira Sullivan, Sonny Stitt, Lou Donaldson, Jimmy Smith, Dewy Redman

Biography Dudley. CLE/BOS 60's, 70's, early '80s Cleveland; '87 - '90s Berklee teacher (Boston). Strong, assertive, yet sensitive. One of the only '70s drummers to explore free playing with a large set. Percussionist. Author: *The Beat, the Body and the Brain* (vols.1 & 2) 1993/4 CPP Belwin.

Album Title	Name of Artist	Label w Number	Date Recorded	Format	Country
Weather Report (drums)	Weather Report	Columbia CK 32494	1974	CD	US
And in this Corner T.L. (perc)	Tom Lellis	Inner City IC 1090	11/79	LP	US

Drummer Discography

Name Hall, Roy   **Birth Date**

Birthplace   **Reference**

Played with Dizzy Gillespie, George Handy, Tony Fruscella, Dave Schildkraut

Biography NYC. Late '40s - '50s made several jazz recordings with artists listed.

Album Title	Name of Artist	Label w Number	Date Recorded	Format	Country
Dizzy Gillespie	Dizzy Gillespie	Phoenix LP4	1945	LP	US
Central Ave.Breakdown	George Handy	Onyx ORI 212	1945	LP	US
First Sessions vol.1	Don Lamphere	Prestige 24114	7/2/49	CD	US
Tony F./Phil Woods quintet	Tony Fruscella	Stateside SJ80117	1955	LP	JA

Name Hamilton, Chico   **Birth Date** 9/21/21

Birthplace LA, CA   **Reference** Grove / Feather ('60s and '70s)

Played with Lester Young, Dexter Gordon, Lionel Hampton, Gerry Mulligan, Eric Dolphy, JimHall

Biography LA. '50s one of first Gerry Mulligan quartet drummers—brush master; Late '50s- '60s leader of own groups,usually quintets (including Eric Dolphy, Jim Hall) Large discography.

Album Title	Name of Artist	Label w Number	Date Recorded	Format	Country
*The Gerry Mulligan Quartet	Gerry Mulligan	Pacific Jazz TOCJ-5411	8/16/52	CD	JA
California Concerts	Gerry Mulligan	Pac. Jazz CDP746860	11/12/54	CD	US
Spectacular	Chico Hamilton	Pacific Jazz PJ1209	8/4/55	LP	US
Chico Hamilton Quintet	Chico Hamilton	Warner BrothersS1344	2/25/59	LP	US

Name Harewood, Al   **Birth Date** 6/3/23

Birthplace New York, NY   **Reference** Grove / Feather ('60s)

Played with J.J. Johnson, Kai Winding, Stan Getz, Lee Konitz, Grant Green, Curtis Fuller

Biography NYC. '60s large, important discography—popular sideman—steady swing, flexible style. Gigi Gryce, Art Farmer, many others; '70s taught at Livingston College, Rutgers; '80s - '90s continues playing career. *Up and Down* is a particularly good example of his work.

Album Title	Name of Artist	Label w Number	Date Recorded	Format	Country
Trombomania	J.J.Johnson & Kai	Affinity 761 Bethlehem	1/25/55	CD	UK
Up at Mintons, vols.1 and 2	Stanley Turrentine	BN TOCJ-4069/4070	2/23/61	2 CDs	JA
*Up and Down	Horace Parlan	BN TOCJ-4082	6/18/61	CD	JA
*Jubilee Shout	Stanley Turrentine	Blue Note CDP784127	10/18/62	CD	US

Name Harris, Beaver   **Birth Date** 4/20/36   12/22/91

Birthplace Pittsburgh, PA   **Reference** Grove / Feather ('70s)

Played with Sonny Rollins, HoraceSilver, Roswell Rudd, Thelonious Monk

Biography NYC. Late '60s - '80s modernist/avant-garde stylist. Composer. Led, recorded own groups: see *Grove* for listing.

Album Title	Name of Artist	Label w Number	Date Recorded	Format	Country
For John Coltrane	Albert Ayler	Impulse AS-9336/2	12/18/66	LP	US
The Village Concerts	Albert Ayler	Impulse MCAD-39123	2/26/67	CD	US
In Concert	Chet Baker	India Navigation1052	1974	CD	US

Drummer Discography

Name Harris, Joe   **Birth Date** 12/23/26

Birthplace Pittsburgh PA   **Reference** Grove / Feather (New)

Played with Charlie Parker, Dizzy Gillespie, Bud Powell, George Russell, Art Farmer, Teddy Charles

Biography NYC.'40s substituted for Roach with Parker quintet at Roost, recorded famous *Carnegie* Parker concert (listed); '50s Billy Eckstine, Lester Young, Garner; '56 moved to Europe; '72 - '86 back: teacher at U. of Pittsburgh. Versatile drummer/percussionist with a large, important discography.

Album Title	Name of Artist	Label w Number	Date Recorded	Format	Country
*Diz and Bird	Charlie Parker	Roulette RCD59026	9/29/47	CD	US/JA
*Bird at the Roost, vols.2 & 3	Charlie Parker	Savoys: ZDS4412/13	1/1/49	2 CDs	US
*Teddy CharlesTentet	Teddy Charles	Atlantic 7 90983-2	1/6/56	CD	US
*George Russell Smalltet	George Russell	RCA 6467-2RB	3/31/56	CD	US

Name Hart, Billy   **Birth Date** 11/29/40

Birthplace Washington, DC   **Reference** Grove / Feather ('70s)

Played with Jimmy Smith, Wes Montgomery, Herbie Hancock, Miles Davis, Stan Getz

Biography aka Jabali. NYC. '60s Jimmy Smith,Wes Montgomery; '70s Herbie Hancock's *Headhunters*, Miles Davis, Stan Getz; '80s - '90s popular, versatile recording artist with large discography. Swinging accompanist. Author: *Jazz Drumming* (Advance).

Album Title	Name of Artist	Label w Number	Date Recorded	Format	Country
*Mwandishi	Herbie Hancock	Warner Bros.SW1898	1970	LP	US
*The Master	Stan Getz	Columbia 467138	10/1/75	CD	AUS
*This is Buck Hill	Buck Hill	SteepleChase 1095	3/20/78	CD	DEN
*Pure Getz	Stan Getz	Concord CCD-4168	1/29/82	CD	US

Name Harte, Roy   **Birth Date** 5/27/24

Birthplace New York, NY   **Reference** Feather ('60s)

Played with Lester Yong, Bud Shank, Bob Enevoldsen, Harry Babasin, Laurindo Almeida

Biography NYC/LA. '40s student of Dave Tough; '50s: Lester Young—then to LA, where he opened a well known drum store in Hollywood *Drum City*—published important drumming books, including Pete Magadini's *Musician's Guide to Polyrhythms* vols.1 and 2 (originally published by *Try*).

Album Title	Name of Artist	Label w Number	Date Recorded	Format	Country
Bud Shank Quartet	Bud Shank	Pacific Jazz 1205	3/1/54	LP	US/JA
Bob Enevoldsen Quintet	BobEnevoldsen	Nocturne NLP6	4/1/54	US	US
Lorraine Geller Memorial	Lorraine Geller	Fresh Sounds 195	7/4/54	CD	SWI
Harry Babasin Quintet	Harry Babasin	Nocturne NLP3	9/23/54	LP	US

Name Hayes, Louis   **Birth Date** 5/31/37

Birthplace Detroit, MI   **Reference** Grove / Feather (All)

Played with Horace Silver, John Coltrane, Julian Adderley, Oscar Peterson, McCoy Tyner

Biography NYC. Mid '50s - '60s large, important discography; '70s - '90s leads own bands. Exciting swing: creates momentum by "tipping" (on top of the beat, with straight quarter notes) on ride cymbal. Hi-hat trade mark: a fast open/close stroke—hand hits on up beat—foot plays the down beat.

Album Title	Name of Artist	Label w Number	Date Recorded	Format	Country
*Six Pieces of Silver	Horace Silver	BlueNote B21Y 81539	11/10/56	CD	US
*Finger Poppin'	Horace Silver	BlueNote B21Y 84008	1/31/59	CD	US
*Cannonball in SanFrancisco	Julian Adderley	RiversideOJCCD-035-2	10/18/59	CD	US
*B. H. at the Jazz Workshop	Barry Harris	RiversideOJCCD-208-2	5/15/60	CD	US

Drummer Discography

Name Haynes, Roy   **Birth Date** 3/13/26

Birthplace Roxbury , MA   **Reference** Grove / Feather (All)

Played with Charlie Parker, Lester Young, Bud Powell, Sarah Vaughn, Stan Getz, John Coltrane

Biography NYC. See pages 35-36 for a more extensive biography. Very large, important discography— live recordings: with Bird (all recommended); with Bud Powell *Birdland '53*, *Fresh Sounds* CD1017; with Thelonious Monk's quartet at *Five Spot* (with Coltrane) *Discovery*, Blue Note B21S-99786.

Album Title	Name of Artist	Label w Number	Date Recorded	Format	Country
*Inner Fires	Bud Powell	Electra Musician 71009	4/5/53	CD	US
*The Sound of Sonny	Sonny Rollins	RiversideOJCCD-092-2	6/11/57	CD	US
*Thelonious In Action	Thelonious Monk	RiversideOJCCD-103-2	7/9/58	CD	US
*Now he Sings, now he Sobs	Chick Corea	Blue Note B21Y 90055	3/14/68	CD	US

Name Heard, J.C.   **Birth Date** 10/8/17

Birthplace Dayton, OH   **Reference** Grove / Feather (New and '70s)

Played with Benny Carter, Coleman Hawkins, Red Norvo, Howard McGhee, JATP

Biography NYC. '40s famous swing bands; '50s recorded for Norman Granz's *Jazz at the Philharmonic* concerts with modern players—Charlie Parker, Lester Young. Large, important discography. Singer and dancer. Loose swing suited for both swing, and early modern jazz styles.

Album Title	Name of Artist	Label w Number	Date Recorded	Format	Country
*Red Norvo's famous jam	Red Norvo	Spotlite 127	6/6/45	LP	UK
*Every Bit of It	Charlie Parker	Spotlite 150D	9/4/45	LP	UK
*The Bebop Revolution	Dizzy Gillespie	RCA 2177 2- RB	2/22/46	CD	US
*Bird:Complete Verve(JATP)	Charlie Parker	Verve 10 837141-2	6/52	10 CD box	US

Name Heath, Albert   **Birth Date** 5/31/35

Birthplace Philadelphia, PA.   **Reference** Grove / Feather (All)

Played with J.J. Johnson, Jazztet, Kenny Dorham, Clifford Jordan, Heath Brothers

Biography aka Tootie/Kuumba. NYC. Late '50s - 60s large, important discography. Brother of Percy, and Jimmy—member Heath brother's band. Popular recording artist—exciting, enthusiastic style.

Album Title	Name of Artist	Label w Number	Date Recorded	Format	Country
*Coltrane	John Coltrane	Prestige OJCCD-020-2	5/31/57	CD	US
*Incredible Jazz Guitar	Wes Montgomery	RiversideOJCCD-036-2	1/26/60	CD	US
*Really Big!	Jimmy Heath	RiversideOJCCD-1799		CD	US
*Spellbound	Clifford Jordan	RiversideOJCCD-766-2	8/10/60	CD	US

Name Higgins, Billy   **Birth Date** 10/11/36

Birthplace LA, CA   **Reference** Grove / Feather (All)

Played with Ornette Coleman, John Coltrane, Art Farmer, Dexter Gordon, Cedar Walton, Clifford Jordan

Biography LA/NYC. Late '50s - '90s very popular recording artist—large, important discography. Elegant, economic, light, and clean style. Buoyant, yet tight cymbal time—use of straight eighth notes for comping. Drums usually high pitched. Versatile small group accompanist—bop/avant-garde.

Album Title	Name of Artist	Label w Number	Date Recorded	Format	Country
*Shape of Jazz to Come	Ornette Coleman	Atlantic 1317-2	5/22/59	CD	US
*Monk at the Blackhawk	Thelonious Monk	RiversideOJCCD-305-2	4/28/60	CD	US
*Go	Dexter Gordon	Blue Note B21Y 46094	8/27/62	CD	US
*A.F. quintet live at Boomers	Art Farmer	East Wind-8042	5/14/76	LP	JA

Drummer Discography

Name Hogan, G.T.　　　　**Birth Date** 1/16/29

Birthplace Galveston, TX.　　　　**Reference** Grove / Feather (New)

Played with Bud Powell, Kenny Dorham, Randy Weston, Elmo Hope

Biography NYC. Late '50s - '60s played, recorded with great modern NYC players, then returned to Texas.

Album Title	Name of Artist	Label w Number	Date Recorded	Format	Country
This is New	Kenny Drew	RiversideOJCCD-483-2	3/28/57	CD	US
Two Horns/Two Rhythm	Kenny Dorham	RiversideOJCCD-463-2	11/13/57	CD	US
Elmo Hope Plays	Elmo Hope	Fresh Sounds 181	1961	CD	SWI
Rollin' with Leo	Leo Parker	Blue Note CDP784095	10/20/61	CD	US

Name Humair, Daniel　　　　**Birth Date** 5/23/38

Birthplace Geneva, Switzerland　　　　**Reference** Grove / Feather ('60s and '70s)

Played with Kenny Dorham, Phil Woods, Chet Baker, Jim Hall, Phil Woods

Biography Europe. Late '50s - '70s played with visiting American jazz players. '80s - '90s own groups. Popular European drummer, large discography—original styles. Painter.

Album Title	Name of Artist	Label w Number	Date Recorded	Format	Country
Barney	Barney Wilen	RCA 2525M	4/24/59	LP	JA
Montreux Jazz Festival	Phil Woods	MGM 2315009	6/1/69	LP	FR
It's Nice to be with You	Jim Hall	MPS 15245	6/27/69	LP	GER
Black Narcissus	Joe Henderson	Milestone M9071	10/1/74	LP	US

Name Humphries, Lex　　　　**Birth Date** 8/22/36

Birthplace Rockaway, NJ　　　　**Reference** Grove / Feather (New)

Played with Dizzy Gillespie, Jazztet, Donald Byrd, Sun Ra, Freddie Hubbard, John Coltrane

Biography NYC. Early '60s Coltrane,Wes Montgomery. Very popular '60s recording artist—large, important discography. Great drummer—strong, swinging momentum—exciting solos. Inactive discography from1965.

Album Title	Name of Artist	Label w Number	Date Recorded	Format	Country
*Giant Steps	John Coltrane	Atlantic 1311-2	4/1/59	CD	US
*Byrd in Flight	Donald Byrd	Blue Note TOCJ-4048	1/25/60	CD	JA
*Meet the Jazztet	Art Farmer	Chess MCA 91550	2/6/60	CD	US
*So Much Guitar	Wes Montgomery	Riverside OJC-233-2	8/4/61	CD	US

Name Humphries, Roger　　　　**Birth Date** 11/30/44

Birthplace Pittsburgh, PA　　　　**Reference** Feather ('60s)

Played with Horace Silver, Carmell Jones

Biography NYC. 1964-'66 Horace Silver quintet. Exciting, energetic time and fills.

Album Title	Name of Artist	Label w Number	Date Recorded	Format	Country
*Song for my Father	Horace Silver	Blue Note B21Y 84185	10/31/64	CD	US
*Cape Verdean Blues	Horace Silver	Blue Note B21Y 84220	10/22/65	CD	US
*Jay Hawk Talk	Carmell Jones	Prestige PR LP 7401	5/8/65	LP	US
*The Jody Grind	Horace Silver	Blue Note B21Y 84250	11/23/66	CD	US

Drummer Discography

Name Hunt, Joe   **Birth Date** 7/31/38

Birthplace Richmond, IN   **Reference**

Played with David Baker, George Russell, John Handy, Stan Getz, Jim Hall, Bill Evans

Biography NYC/BOS. '50s studied in Indianapolis—Willis Kirk (author: *Brush Fire*), IU—Richard Johnson; '60s NYC Russell, Getz, Evans; '70s - '90s Boston, Berklee since '71— own groups (Mike Stern, John Scofield). Additional Russell recordings: *Riverside* OJCCD-365; *Decca* LPs: 4183; 9220.

Album Title	Name of Artist	Label w Number	Date Recorded	Format	Country
*Stratusphunk	George Russell	Riverside314 (OJC232)	10/18/60	LP	US
*Ezzthetics	George Russell	RiversideOJCCD-070-2	5/8/61	CD	US
A Day in the City	Don Friedman	RiversideOJCCD-1775	6/12/61	CD	US
*Getz /Gilberto #2	Stan Getz	Verve 314 519 800-2	10/9/64	CD	US

Name Igoe, Sonny   **Birth Date** 10/8/23

Birthplace Jersey City, NJ   **Reference** Grove / Feather (New)

Played with Charlie Ventura, Woody Herman, Benny Goodman, Chuck Wayne

Biography NYC.'50s big band and small group bop recordings. Recently, active as a teacher in NJ.

Album Title	Name of Artist	Label w Number	Date Recorded	Format	Country
*Light Gray (one title)	Wardell Gray	Cool 'N Blue CD 116	1948	CD	SWI
*Early Atumn	Woody Herman	Discovery DSCD-944	5/30/52	CD	US
Charlie Ventura Quartet	Charlie Ventura	Verve MG V 8143	1954	LP	US
The Four Most Guitars	Chuck Wayne	ABC Paramount 109	1956	LP	US

Name Inzalaco,Tony   **Birth Date** 1/14/38

Birthplace Passaic, NJ   **Reference** Feather ('70s)

Played with Maynard Ferguson, Donald Byrd, Dexter Gordon, Art Farmer, Horace Parlan

Biography NYC/Europe. '60s Ferguson, Byrd; '70s active in Europe. '80s - '90s Boston/LA. Powerful, swinging drummer.

Album Title	Name of Artist	Label w Number	Date Recorded	Format	Country
A Sleeping Bee	Art Farmer	Sonet SNTF 715	1/4/74	LP	SWE
Stable Mable	Dexter Gordon	SteepleChase 1040	3/10/75	LP	DEN
No Blues	Horace Parlan	SteepleChase 1056	12/10/75	LP	DEN

Name Isola, Frank   **Birth Date** 2/20/25

Birthplace Detroit, MI   **Reference** Grove / Feather (New)

Played with Charlie Parker, Stan Getz, Gerry Mulligan, Bob Brookmeyer, Mose Allison

Biography NYC. Early '50s major recording period—important discography— '57 returned to Detroit with little recording since. Original modern drummer with traditional roots (Baby Dodds influence). Linear solo style— transcribed by Alan Dawson: *Manual for the Modern Drummer*.

Album Title	Name of Artist	Label w Number	Date Recorded	Format	Country
*Early Stan	Stan Getz	PrestigeOJCCD-654-2	12/12/52	CD	US
*Stan Getz 57	Stan Getz	Verve 23 MV3181	7/30/53	LP	JA
*Interpretations	Stan Getz	Verve POJJ -1512	7/30/53	LP	JA
The Fabulous Gerry Mulligan	Gerry Mulligan	Vogue 651 600028	6/1/54	CD	FR

Drummer Discography

Name Jackson, Oliver   **Birth Date** 4/28/33

Birthplace Detroit, MI   **Reference** Grove

Played with Earl Hines, Buck Clayton, Benny Goodman, Thad Jones, Tommy Flanagan, Dexter Gordon

Biography NYC. '50s - '90s Traditional and modern styles—solid swing.

Album Title	Name of Artist	Label w Number	Date Recorded	Format	Country
Other Sounds	Yusef Lateef	New JazzOJCCD-399-2	10/11/57	CD	US
Cry Tender	Yusef Lateef	New JazzOJCCD-482-2	10/16/59	CD	US
Bad Bossa Nova	Gene Ammons	Prestige OJCCD-351-2	9/9/62	CD	US
At Montreux with Jr. Mance	Dexter Gordon	Prestige PRCD-7861-2	1981	LP	US

Name James, Billy   **Birth Date** 4/20/36

Birthplace Pittsburgh, PA   **Reference** Grove / Feather ('60s)

Played with Don Patterson, Gene Ammons, Sonny Stitt, James Moody

Biography NYC. '50s Lionel Hampton, Booker Ervin; '60s Eddie Davis, Eric Kloss. Loose, swinging time. Ammons LP, with Sonny Stitt, was reissued as a double LP set: *Prime Cuts* Verve 2V65-8812

Album Title	Name of Artist	Label w Number	Date Recorded	Format	Country
Boss Tenors in Orbit	Gene Ammons	Verve MGV8468	2/19/62	LP	US
Introducing Eric Kloss	Eric Kloss	Prestige PR 7442	9/1/65	LP	US
The Boss Men	Don Patterson	Prestige PR 7466	12/28/65	LP	US
*Boppin' and Burnin'	Don Patterson	Prestige PR 7563	2/22/68	LP	US

Name Jarvis, Clifford   **Birth Date** 8/26/41

Birthplace Boston, MA   **Reference** Grove / Feather ('70s)

Played with Roland Kirk, Barry Harris, Grant Green, Freddie Hubbard, Jackie McLean, Sun Ra

Biography NYC. '60s with artists listed. Very exciting bop drummer— important discography. High spirited accompaniment and solos.

Album Title	Name of Artist	Label w Number	Date Recorded	Format	Country
*Open Sesame	Freddie Hubbard	Blue Note CDP7 84040	6/19/60	CD	US
*Newer than New	Barry Harris	Riverside RLP 413	9/28/61	LP	US
*Chasin' the Bird	Barry Harris	Riverside VIJ-149	5/3/62	LP	JA
*Hub Tones	Freddie Hubbard	Blue Note B21Y 84115	10/10/62	CD	US

Name Jefferson, Ron   **Birth Date** 2/13/26

Birthplace New York, NY   **Reference** Grove / Feather (New)

Played with Coleman Hawkins, Oscar Pettiford, Lester Young, Les McCann, Carmell Jones

Biography NYC/LA. Early '50s swing bands— Roy Eldridge, Hawkins; late '50s recorded with modern groups, member of *The Jazz Modes* (57-59); '59— to California, several recordings with McCann. Nice brushes. Remains active, leading own recording groups.

Album Title	Name of Artist	Label w Number	Date Recorded	Format	Country
*Bass	Oscar Pettiford	Bethlhem COCY-7722	1954	CD	JA
Piano: East/West	Freddie Redd	Prestige OJCCD-1705	2/28/55	CD	US
Leroy Walks Again	Leroy Vinnegar	Contem. OJCCD-454-2	8/1/61	CD	US
Business Meetin'	Carmell Jones	Pacific Jazz LP 53	1962	LP	US

Drummer Discography

Name Johnson, Gus   **Birth Date** 11/15/13

Birthplace Tyler, TX   **Reference** Grove / Feather (All)

Played with Jay McShann, Charlie Parker, Count Basie, Earl Hines, Stan Getz, Oscar Pettiford

Biography NYC. Early '40s Jay McShann band (with Bird); '50s Basie, Gerry Mulligan, Zoot Sims. Solid (Basie-like) swing —combined with early modern influence. Popular recording artist—mostly mainstream/big band jazz. All Basie *Verve* records are recommended, but most are out of print.

Album Title	Name of Artist	Label w Number	Date Recorded	Format	Country
*Early Bird	Jay McShann	Stash CD 542	11/30/40	CD	US
*The Count	Count Basie	Verve MGV-8070	1955	LP	US
*G. Mulligan: Arranger	Gerry Mulligan	Sony Col. 468411 2	4/19/57	CD	AUS
*Oscar Pettiford Orchestra	Oscar Pettiford	ABC Paramount227	8/23/57	LP	US

Name Johnson, Osie   **Birth Date** 1/11/23   2/10/66

Birthplace Washington, DC   **Reference** Grove / Feather (New and '60s)

Played with Earl Hines, Coleman Hawkins,Sonny Stitt, Al Cohn, Zoot Sims, Gil Evans

Biography James. NYC. '40s - '60s Very large, important discography. Known for NYC jazz studio work and association with bassist, Milt Hinton. His basic approach utilized swing techniques (rolls etc.)—in some ways similar to Kenny Clarke (his contemporary). Composer, arranger, and singer.

Album Title	Name of Artist	Label w Number	Date Recorded	Format	Country
*RCA Victor Jazz Worshop	George Russell	RCA 6471-2 - RB	3/3/56	CD	US
*Street Swingers	Bob Brookmeyer	Pacific Jazz WP 1239	12/13/57	LP	US
*Legrand Jazz	Michel Legrand	Philips 32 JD 159	6/30/58	CD	JA
*Into the Hot	Gil Evans	Impulse 32XD-612	10/31/61	CD	JA

Name Johnson, Sonny   **Birth Date**

Birthplace   **Reference**

Played with Wes Montgomery, Lionel Hampton, Art Farmer

Biography Robert. IN '50s drummer with the first Montgomery brothers band in Indianapolis.

Album Title	Name of Artist	Label w Number	Date Recorded	Format	Country
Art Farmer Septet	Art Farmer	PrestigeOJCCD-054-2	7/2/53	CD	US
Almost Forgotten	Wes Montgomery	Columbia FC 30509	6/15/55	LP	US

Name Johnston, Clarence   **Birth Date**

Birthplace   **Reference**

Played with Sonny Stitt, James Moody, Jimmy Forrest, Phineas Newborn

Biography NYC. '50s popular swinging jazz/blues drummer; early '60s *Blue Note* LPs for Freddie Roach.

Album Title	Name of Artist	Label w Number	Date Recorded	Format	Country
Hi Fi Party	James Moody	Prestige OJCCD-1780	8/23/55	CD	US
Wail, Moody, Wail	James Moody	Prestige OJCCD-1791	12/12/55	CD	US
Most, Much	Jimmy Forrest	Prestige OJCCD-350-2	10/19/61	CD	US
P. N. Live in Osaka Japan	Phineas Newborn	Phillips RJ-7420	9/5/77	LP	JA

Drummer Discography

Name Jones, Al   **Birth Date** 12/18/30   c. 1976

Birthplace Philadelphia, PA.   **Reference** Grove

Played with Dizzy Gillespie, Miles Davis, Joe Carroll, Milt Jackson, Billie Holiday, Dexter Gordon

Biography NYC/Europe. Early '50s recorded with Gillespie—with him in Europe; '62 moved to Belgium.

Album Title	Name of Artist	Label w Number	Date Recorded	Format	Country
School Days	Dizzy Gillespie	Savoy SV-0157	8/9/51	CD	JA
*The Champ	Dizzy Gillespie	Savoy SV-0170	10/25/51	CD	JA
Dizzy in Paris	Dizzy Gillespie	Vogue 33324	2/22/53	LP	FR
The Bebop Pianists	Wade Legge	Vogue VDJ-574	2/27/53	LP	FR

Name Jones, Elvin   **Birth Date** 9/9/27

Birthplace Pontiac, MI   **Reference** Grove / Feather (All)

Played with Thad Jones, Pepper Adams, Donald Byrd, J.J. Johnson, John Coltrane, *Jazz Machine*

Biography NYC. See pages 44-48 for a more extensive biography. Selected discography here represents his early work in late '50s. All '60s recordings with John Coltrane are recommended, and—his sideman dates during that time, see page 44. Also—J.J. Johnson's *J is for Jazz* Col. LP-935.

Album Title	Name of Artist	Label w Number	Date Recorded	Format	Country
*Dial J.J.	J.J. Johnson	Sony 32 DP 594	1/31/57	CD	JA
*Overseas	Tommy Flanagan	DIW 305 CD	8/15/57	CD	JA
*10 to 4 at the Five Spot	Pepper Adams	RiversideOJCCD-031-2	4/5/58	CD	US
*Live at the Village Vanguard	John Coltrane	MCAD 39136	11/2/61	CD	US

Name Jones, Harold   **Birth Date** 2/27/40

Birthplace Richmond, IN.   **Reference** Grove / Feather ('70s)

Played with Count Basie, Sarah Vaughn, Benny Carter

Biography CHI/LA. Versatile, swinging drummer. '67 - '72 Count Basie (several recordings); '80s Sarah Vaughn; '90s active—recording in LA area.

Album Title	Name of Artist	Label w Number	Date Recorded	Format	Country
Playin' for Keeps	Bunky Green	Argo LP 766	1/18/66	LP	US
Straight Ahead	Count Basie	Dot 25902	1968	LP	US
B. C., Alive and Well in Japan	Benny Carter	PL 2308216	1977	LP	US
Summer Strut	Andy Simpkins	Discovery DS 892	6/21/83	LP	US

Name Jones, Jo   **Birth Date** 10/7/11   9/3/85

Birthplace Chicago, IL   **Reference** Grove / Feather (New and '70s)

Played with Count Basie, Lester Young, Gene Ammons, Sonny Stitt, Ray Bryant, JATP

Biography Jonathan "Papa Jo" Jones. NYC. '30s - '40s great swing drummer who influenced early modern styles—innovative use of the high hat with Count Basie in late '30s (All Basie recordings recommended), remained active until '85. See *Drummin' Men* (Korall) for a more extensive bio.

Album Title	Name of Artist	Label w Number	Date Recorded	Format	Country
*All Star Sessions with S.Stitt	Gene Ammons	Prestige OJCCD-014-2	3/5/50	CD	US
*S.Stitt Plays Quincy Jones	Sonny Stitt	Roost LP 2204	9/30/55	LP	US
*Sonny Rollins/Thad Jones	Thad Jones	Zeta EPM ZET 704	12/12/56	CD	FR
*New York Jazz	Sonny Stitt	Verve MGV8219	1957	LP	US

Drummer Discography

Name Jones, "Philly" Joe   **Birth Date** 7/15/23   8/30/85

Birthplace Philadelphia, PA   **Reference** Grove / Feather (All)

Played with Tony Scott, Miles Davis, Bill Evans, Tadd Dameron, Sonny Rollins

Biography NYC. See pages 40-43 for a more extensive bio. Also recommended: all Miles Davis recordings for *Columbia* and *Prestige*. The Complete Miles Davis on *Prestige* is available in an 8 CD box set, *Chronicle* (8PRCD-012-2). In addition, he recorded hundreds of fine sessions as a sideman.

Album Title	Name of Artist	Label w Number	Date Recorded	Format	Country
*Tenor Madness	Sonny Rollins	Prestige OJCCD-124-2	5/24/56	CD	US
*Milestones	Miles Davis	Columbia CK 40837	4/2/58	CD	US
*Blues for Dracula	Philly Joe Jones	RiversideOJCCD-230-2	9/17/58	CD	US
*Drums Around the World	Philly Joe Jones	RiversideOJCCD-1792	5/4/59	CD	US

Name Jones, Willie   **Birth Date** 10/20/29

Birthplace New York, NY   **Reference** Grove / Feather ('60s)

Played with Charlie Parker, J.J. Johnson, Kenny Dorham, Charles Mingus, Thelonious Monk

Biography NYC. '50s popular jazz drummer—with the outstanding modern artists listed.

Album Title	Name of Artist	Label w Number	Date Recorded	Format	Country
*T.Monk and Sonny Rollins	Thelonious Monk	Prestige OJCCD -059-2	11/13/53	CD	US
*Monk	Thelonious Monk	Prestige OJCCD -016-2	11/13/53	CD	US
Meditations	Elmo Hope	Prestige OJCCD 1751	7/28/55	CD	US
Pithecanthropus Erectus	Charles Mingus	Atlantic 8809-2	1/30/56	CD	US

Name Kahn, Tiny   **Birth Date** c.1923   8/19/53

Birthplace New York, NY   **Reference** Grove / Feather (New)

Played with Boyd Raeburn, Georgie Auld, Lester Young, Stan Getz, Charlie Barnet

Biography Norman. NYC. Late '40s - '53 composer, arranger—many famous bop arrangements—Elliot Lawrence, Woody Herman,Charlie Barnet. Light touch, swinging, original stylist. Solos are rare—linear /syncopated—*Getz at Storyville*. A favorite in big bop bands of late '40s - early '50s.

Album Title	Name of Artist	Label w Number	Date Recorded	Format	Country
*Early Bebop	Red Rodney	Mercury 830 922-2	1/29/47	CD	JA
*The Bebop Era	Chubby Jackson	Columbia CK40972	2/24/49	CD	US
*Cohn's Tones	Al Cohn	Savoy SV- 0187	7/29/50	CD	JA
*Getz at Storyville	Stan Getz	Capitol B21Y 96052	10/28/51	CD	US

Name Kay, Connie   **Birth Date** 4/27/27

Birthplace Tuckahoe, NY   **Reference** Grove / Feather (All)

Played with Lester Young, Charlie Parker, MJQ, Stan Getz, Benny Goodman

Biography NYC. '50s joined MJQ in 1955—remained their drummer since; 60s popular accompanist. Large, important discography. Steady, strong swing.

Album Title	Name of Artist	Label w Number	Date Recorded	Format	Country
*Plenty, Plenty Soul	Milt Jackson	Atlantic 1269-2	1/5/57	CD	US
*Stan Getz and J.J. Johnson	Stan Getz	Verve 8311 272-2	10/19/57	CD	US
*MJQ with Sonny Rollins	MJQ	Atlantic 30XD-1012	8/3/58	CD	JA
*Bags and Trane	Milt Jackson	Atlantic 1368-2	1/15/59	CD	US

Drummer Discography

Name Kluger, Irv   **Birth Date** 7/9/21

Birthplace Brooklyn, NY   **Reference** Grove / Feather (New)

Played with George Auld, Bud Powell, Dizzy Gillespie, Stan Kenton, Buddy DeFranco

Biography NYC/LA. '40s active during early NY modern movement (especially big bands); '50s - '60s LA studios, co-owner, with Roy Harte of *Drum City*, one of the first exclusive drum stores. *Dizzy Gillespie:The Development of an American Artist* order from Smithsonian Museum, Wash. DC.

Album Title	Name of Artist	Label w Number	Date Recorded	Format	Country
*Groovin' High	Dizzy Gillespie	Savoy SV-0152	2/9/45	CD	JA
*Dizzy Gillespie: The Devel...	George Auld(1 title)	Colum. R004 P2 13455	3/28/45	2 LPs	US
*Shaw Nuff'	Bud Powell	Xanadu FDC 5167	5/2/45	CD	FR
*Jazz into Cool	Buddy DeFranco	Capitol TOCJ-5700	4/23/49	CD	JA

Name LaBarbera, Joe   **Birth Date** 2/22/48

Birthplace Mount Morris, NY   **Reference** Grove/ Feather ('70s)

Played with Woody Herman, Bob Brookmeyer, Bill Evans, Jim Hall

Biography NYC. '70s Chuck Mangione, Bob Brookmeyer, Pat Labarbera (brother), Bill Evans trio from 1978 - '80 (when Evans died); '80s Tony Bennett. Loose, swinging drummer—big band and small groups. Strong soloist—influenced by Max Roach and Elvin Jones *We Will Meet Again*.

Album Title	Name of Artist	Label w Number	Date Recorded	Format	Country
Bob Brookmeyer small band	Bob Brookmeyer	Gryphon 628479DX	7/28/78	LPs	US
*We Will Meet Again	Bill Evans	Warner Bros. HS 3411	8/6/79	LP	US
*Concert in Buenos Aries	Bill Evans	Jazz lab vol. 2	9/27/79	CD	Swiss
*The Paris Concert edition 1	Bill Evans	Electra 28P2 2478	11/26/79	CD	JA

Name Lamond, Don   **Birth Date** 8/18/20

Birthplace Oklahoma City, OK   **Reference** Grove / Feather (New)

Played with Woody Herman, Serge Chaloff, Charlie Parker, Stan Getz, Chubby Jackson

Biography NYC. '40s - '50s important big band drummer known for solid time. Replaced Dave Tough with 2nd Woody Herman Herd. Large, important discography. Good example of late '40s big band bop drumming—surprise cadences (bass drum "bombs")—linear fills between bass and snare.

Album Title	Name of Artist	Label w Number	Date Recorded	Format	Country
*The Thundering Herds	Woody Herman	Columbia CK44108	2/19/45	CD	US
*Bird on Dial (complete)	Charlie Parker	Stash STCD567/8/9/10	2/26/47	4 CD Box	US
*Keeper of the Flame	Woody Herman	Capitol CDP798453	12/29/48	CD	US
*Gerry Mulligan/C. Jackson	Chubby Jackson	Prestige OJCCD 711 2	3/15/50	CD	US

Name Landers, Wes   **Birth Date** 1925   2/93

Birthplace Bermuda   **Reference** Grove

Played with Earl Hines, Count Basie, Gene Ammons, Sonny Stitt, Buddy DeFranco, Sonny Clark

Biography CHI/NYC. '50s popular bop accompanist with the outstanding artists listed.

Album Title	Name of Artist	Label w Number	Date Recorded	Format	Country
*The G.Ammons story 78	Gene Ammons	Prestige 24058	7/27/50	CD	US
*First Sessions vol. 2	Sonny Stitt	Prestige 24115	10/8/50	CD	US
Odalisque	Buddy DeFranco	Verve 2527	9/28/53	LP	US
*Blues in the Night	Sonny Clark	Blue Note GXK8156	5/2/58	LP	JA

Drummer Discography

Name La Roca, Pete   **Birth Date** 4/7/38

Birthplace New York, NY   **Reference** Grove / Feather (New and '60s)

Played with Stan Getz, John Coltrane, Sonny Rollins, Paul Bley, Art Farmer, Jackie McLean

Biography Sims. NYC. Late '50s - '60s important late modernist with artists listed—loose, free-wheeling style—original, innovative drum solos. Large, important discography—own records. Composer, leader of own groups (C. Corea, S.Kuhn, S.Swallow, John Gilmore). Recently active, own band.

Album Title	Name of Artist	Label w Number	Date Recorded	Format	Country
*A Night at the Vanguard	Sonny Rollins	Blue Note B21Y 81542	11/3/57	CD	US
*Footloose	Paul Bley	Savoy SV-0140	8/17/62	CD	JA
*Sing Me Softly of Blues	Art Farmer	Atlantic P-81038A	3/12/65	LP	JA
*Turkish Women at the Baths	Pete La Roca	Douglas SD 782	5/25/67	LP	US

Name Lee, David Jr.   **Birth Date** 1/4/41

Birthplace New Orleans, LA   **Reference** Grove

Played with Dizzy Gillespie, Roy Ayers, Joe Newman, Sonny Rollins, Charlie Rouse

Biography New Orleans. 1969 Dizzy Gillespie; '70s Roy Ayers, Sonny Rollins ('72 -'75). Composer—see *Strata-East* 660.51.012

Album Title	Name of Artist	Label w Number	Date Recorded	Format	Country
Next Album	Sonny Rollins	Milestone OJCCD-312	7/1/72	CD	US
Horn Culture	Sonny Rollins	Milestone OJCCD-314	7/1/73	CD	US
*Two is One	Charlie Rouse	Strata-East 660.51.012	1974	CD	GER
The Cutting Edge	Sonny Rollins	Milestone OJCCD-468	7/6/74	CD	US

Name Leighton, Elaine   **Birth Date** 5/22/26

Birthplace New York, NY   **Reference** Feather (New)

Played with Beryl Booker, Jimmy Raney, Jackie Cain, Roy Kral, Billie Holiday

Biography NYC. Mid '50s with artists listed, *Cats versus Chicks* 10" *MGM* LP listed (with Kenny Clarke) is very rare and out of print. Also recorded with Beryl Booker: *MGM* and *Cadet*.

Album Title	Name of Artist	Label w Number	Date Recorded	Format	Country
Billie's Blues	Billie Holiday	Capitol B21Y 48786	1/5/54	CD	US
*J. Raney and Sonny Clark	Jimmy Raney	Xanadu BRJ-4542	1/13/54	CD	JA
*Cats versus Chicks	Various artists	MGM E3614	6/2/54	LP	US

Name Levey, Stan   **Birth Date** 4/5/25

Birthplace Philadelphia, PA   **Reference** Grove / Feather (All)

Played with Dizzy Gillespie, Oscar Pettiford, Charlie Parker, Thelonious Monk, Dexter Gordon, Stan Kenton

Biography NYC/LA. Mid '40s one of the first modern drummers active on 52nd Street; '50s Kenton, moved to LA (large important discography there—Conte Candoli, Frank Rosolino, Dexter Gordon, own albums—strong, dominant accompanist); Photographer—several jazz album cover photos.

Album Title	Name of Artist	Label w Number	Date Recorded	Format	Country
*Smithsonian Collection	Dizzy Gillespie	Columbia P2 13455	2/7/46	LP	US
*New Concepts	Stan Kenton	Capitol B21Y 92865	9/8/52	CD	US
*Stanley the Steamer	Stan Levey	Affinity 768 Bethlehem	12/6/54	CD	UK
*For Musicians Only	Dizzy Gillespie	Verve 837 435-2	10/15/56	CD	US

Drummer Discography

Name Levitt, Alan   **Birth Date** 1/11/32

Birthplace New York, NY   **Reference** Grove / Feather (New)

Played with Charlie Parker, Charlie Mingus, Stan Getz, Lennie Tristano, Paul Bley

Biography NYC/Europe. '50s played with major NYC jazz figures '60s moved to France and has become active in Europe since. Original style, strong, yet subtle swing—popular modern accompanist—intersting soloist. Large, important discography.

Album Title	Name of Artist	Label w Number	Date Recorded	Format	Country
Cool Sounds (one title)	Stan Getz	Verve MGV8200	1/5/54	LP	US
*The Paul Bley Trio	Paul Bley	EmArcy MG 36092	2/3/54	LP	US/JA
*Warne Marsh, Lee Konitz	Lee Konitz	Storyville LP 4026	12/27/75	LP	US
*Lee K. Meets Warne Marsh	Lee Konitz	PAUSA 7019	5/24/76	LP	US

Name Lewis, Mel   **Birth Date** 5/10/29   2/2/90

Birthplace Buffalo, NY   **Reference** Grove / Feather (All)

Played with Boyd Raeburn, Stan Kenton, Dizzy Gillespie, Thad Jones, Sonny Stitt

Biography Sokoloff. LA/NYC. '50s Kenton, California recordings; '60s active NY studios, co-leader of big band with Thad Jones '65 - '79, became sole leader; '70s - '80s very popular studio artist with a large, important discography. Relaxed style. Author: big band chart reading/drumming book.

Album Title	Name of Artist	Label w Number	Date Recorded	Format	Country
*Art Pepper plus Eleven	Art Pepper	Contem.OJCCD-341-2	3/14/59	CD	US
*Saxophone Supremacy	Sonny Stitt	Verve UMV 2687	12/1/59	LP	JA
*Big Band in a Jazz Orbit	Bill Holman	VSOP 25		CD	US
*The Concert Jazz Band	Gerry Mulligan	Verve 838 933-2	7/25/60	CD	US

Name Lewis, Victor   **Birth Date**

Birthplace   **Reference**

Played with Dexter Gordon, George Russell, Stan Getz, Smithsonian Jazz Masterworks Orchestra

Biography NYC. '70s Dexter Gordon, Stan Getz; '80s Charles Mingus "Epitaph" orchestra. Buoyant, swinging drummer—versatile, solid, and supportive. His important discography began in '70s.

Album Title	Name of Artist	Label w Number	Date Recorded	Format	Country
Live in the Time Spiral	George Russell	Soul Note 1049CD	7/30/82	CD	JA/IT
*Sophisticated Giant	Dexter Gordon	Columbia CBS 467181	6/21/77	CD	AUS
*Anniversary	Stan Getz	EmArcy 838 769	7/6/87	CD	US
*Serenity	Stan Getz	EmArcy 838 770	7/6/87	CD	US

Name Littman, Peter   **Birth Date** 5/8/35

Birthplace Medford, MA   **Reference** Feather (New)

Played with Chet Baker, Dick Twardzik, Charlie Mariano

Biography BOS/LA.'50s interesting Boston drummer— traveled LA, Europe with Chet Baker. Made no recordings after late '50s, but his small discography is impressive. Interesting soloist—often polyrhythmic.

Album Title	Name of Artist	Label w Number	Date Recorded	Format	Country
*Richard Twardzik 1954	Richard Twardzik	New Artists 1006	1954	CD	US
*Trio R.T./Russ Freeman	Richard Twardzik	Pacific Jazz CJ28 5157	12/1/54	CD	JA
Chet Baker and Crew	Chet Baker	Pac. Jazz B21S-81205	7/31/56	CD	US
Chet Baker Big Band	Chet Baker	PJCDP077778120124	10/26/56	CD	US

Drummer Discography

Name Locke, Eddie   **Birth Date** 2/8/30

Birthplace Detroit, MI   **Reference** Grove

Played with Roy Eldridge, Earl Hines, Coleman Hawkins, Kenny Burrell, Duke Ellington, Lee Konitz

Biography NYC. '60s - '90s (recorded with Ellington '62) popular mainstream accommanist to artists listed.

Album Title	Name of Artist	Label w Number	Date Recorded	Format	Country
Little Susie	Ray Bryant	Columbia CL 1449	1/19/60	LP	US
Hawkins Alive at Village Gate	Coleman Hawkins	Verve 314-513755-2	8/13/62	CD	US
Bluesy Burrell	Kenny Burrell	Moodsville MVLP 29	9/14/62	LP	US
Mexican Bandit Meets Pirate	Paul Gonsalves	Fantasty OJCCD-751-2	8/24/73	CD	US

Name Lovelace, Jimmy   **Birth Date**

Birthplace Kansas City, MO   **Reference**

Played with Eddie Vinson, Wes Montgomery, Junior Mance, Tony Scott

Biography NYC. '60s Wes Montgomery—original, loose swinging drummer—good soloist; hasn't recorded much since 1970.

Album Title	Name of Artist	Label w Number	Date Recorded	Format	Country
*'Round Midnight	Wes Montgomery	Affinity (Charly)13	3/27/65	CD	FR
*Wes Montgomery	Wes Montgomery	FCD 108	3/27/65	CD	FR
*Straight, No Chaser	Wes Montgomery	Bandstand BDCD 1504	3/65	CD	IT

Name Lovelle, Herbie   **Birth Date** 6/1/24

Birthplace New York, NY   **Reference** Grove / Feather (New)

Played with Earl Hines, Buck Clayton, Art Farmer, Sonny Stitt

Biography NYC. '50s - '80s versatile mainstream drummer—big bands, small groups. Pop/blues, studio artist and producer.

Album Title	Name of Artist	Label w Number	Date Recorded	Format	Country
*Early Art	Art Farmer	Prestige NJ 8258	11/9/54	LP	US
Sonny Stitt Quartet	Sonny Stitt	Roost 2252	1963	LP	US
Soul Classics	Sonny Stitt	Prestige OJCCD-6003	9/17/63	CD	US

Name Mann, Howie   **Birth Date** 8/4/27

Birthplace New York, NY   **Reference** Feather ('60s)

Played with Elliot Lawrence, Tony Fruscella, Bobby Scott, Phil Urso

Biography Howard. NYC. '50s active big band and small group drummer.

Album Title	Name of Artist	Label w Number	Date Recorded	Format	Country
*Gerry Mulligan, Arranger	Eliot Lawrence	Columbia 468411-2	4/13/49	CD	AUS
Bebop Revisited vol. 2	Tony Fruscella	Xanadu 172	2/16/52	LP	US
*Philosophy of Phil Urso	Phil Urso	Savoy MG12056	4/4/53	LP	US

Drummer Discography

Name Manne, Shelly   **Birth Date** 6/11/20   9/26/84

Birthplace New York, NY   **Reference** Grove / Feather (All)

Played with Coleman Hawkins, Charlie Parker, Stan Kenton, Woody Herman, Thelonious Monk, Bill Evans

Biography Sheldon. NYC/LA. '40s early roots in trad. NYC jazz; '50s leader west coast jazz styles, own band *Manne's Men* ; '60s own jazz club *Manne Hole*, studio expert. Very important drummer. Versatile—imaginative solos. Large, important discog. First mod. set transcriptions (OJC-152).

Album Title	Name of Artist	Label w Number	Date Recorded	Format	Country
*The Birth of the Cool vol.2	Shorty Rogers	Capitol B21Y 98935	10/8/51	CD	US
*S. Manne and his men vol.1	Shelly Manne	Contem.OJCCD-152-2	4/6/53	CD	US
*The Immortal Clifford Brown	Clifford Brown	Pac.Jazz B21Y 46850	7/12/54	CD	US
*Empathy/A Simple Matter	Bill Evans	Verve 837 757-2	8/14/62	CD	US

Name Marable, Lawrence   **Birth Date** 5/21/29

Birthplace LA, CA   **Reference** Grove / Feather (New)

Played with Stan Getz, Hamp.Hawes, Charlie Parker, Chetr Baker, SonnyStitt, Dexter Gordon

Biography LA. '50s important leader of west coast modern drumming (with Manne, Stan Levey, and Frank Butler). A west coast Art Blakey—strong relaxed swing. Large, important discography. '90s Charlie Haden group.

Album Title	Name of Artist	Label w Number	Date Recorded	Format	Country
* Daddy Plays the Horn	Dexter Gordon	Bethlehem BR5006	9/18/55	CD	JA
*Talkin' and Walkin'	Kenny Drew	Blue Note B21Y 84439	11/18/55	CD	US
* Introducing Carl Perkins	Carl Perkins	Fresh Sounds 010	1/1/56	CD	SP
*Tenorman	Larry Marable	Blue Note B21Y 84440	8/1/56	CD	US

Name Mardigan, Art   **Birth Date** 2/12/23   8/77

Birthplace Detroit, MI   **Reference** Grove / Feather (New)

Played with Dexter Gordon, Fats Navarro, Stan Getz, Wardell Gray, Woody Herman

Biography NYC. Late '40s - '50s important bopdrummer. Steady, relaxed, cymbal time, reminiscent of Shadow Wilson, similarly known for his time playing, rather than solos. Important discography. Returned to Detroit '63— little recording since. Own LP '54 *The Jazz School* EmArcy MG36093.

Album Title	Name of Artist	Label w Number	Date Recorded	Format	Country
*Dexter's Mood	Dexter Gordon	Cool 'N Blue CD114	12/22/47	CD	SWI
*Wardell Gray Memorial vol.2	Wardell Gray	Prestige OJCCD-051-2	5/25/50	CD	US
*Handyland USA (RCA)	George Handy	FreshSoundsNL45959	8/16/54	LP	SP
*Getz at the Shrine	Stan Getz	Verve POCJ-1904	11/8/54	CD	JA

Name Marshall, Eddie   **Birth Date** 4/13/38

Birthplace Springfield, MA   **Reference** Grove

Played with Charlie Mariano, Ahmad Jamal, Dexter Gordon, Stan Getz, Red Garland

Biography SF. '60s East coast— then CA late '60s - '90s. Swinging time. '68-'70 *Fourth Way* (jazz/fusion).

Album Title	Name of Artist	Label w Number	Date Recorded	Format	Country
Toshiko Akiyosi & C. Mariano	Charlie Mariano	Candid 9012	12/5/60	CD	GER
Groovin' Live	Red Garland	Alpha Jazz ALCR-97/8	3/7/77	2 CDs	JA
Dance of the Sun	Eddie Marshall	Timeless CD SJP 109	1989	CD	DU

Drummer Discography

Name Martin, Stu   **Birth Date**

Birthplace   **Reference**

Played with Quincy Jones, Slide Hampton, Sonny Rollins, Lee Konitz, Curtis Fuller

Biography NYC. '60s active NYC player. Strong time. There are rumors of his death in the '70s.

Album Title	Name of Artist	Label w Number	Date Recorded	Format	Country
Boss of soul stream trombne. Curtis Fuller		Warwick 20ED 5072	12/1/60	CD	JA
Great wide world of Q. J: Live Quincy Jones		Mercury 822 613-2	3/10/61	CD	JA
*The Standard Sonny Rollins Sonny Rollins		RCA R25J-1012	6/11/64	CD	JA

Name McBrowne, Lenny   **Birth Date** 1/24/33

Birthplace New York, NY   **Reference** Grove / Feather ('60s and '70s)

Played with Ernie Henry, Sonny Rollins, Sonny Stitt, Sarah Vaughn, Barry Harris, Red Garland

Biography LA/NYC. Late '50s - '60s popular, swinging drummer, with many important artists—substantial discography, including own recordings.

Album Title	Name of Artist	Label w Number	Date Recorded	Format	Country
Lennie McBrowne & 4 souls	Lenny McBrowne	Pacific Jazz 1	9/1/59	LP	US
Eastern Lights	Lenny McBrowne	Riverside RLP346	10/13/60	LP	US
*Luminescence	Barry Harris	Prestige 7498	4/20/67	LP	US
The Quota	Red Garland	MPS 21.20909	5/3/71	LP	GER

Name McCall, Steve   **Birth Date** 9/30/33

Birthplace Chicago, IL   **Reference** Grove

Played with Dexter Gordon, Cecil Taylor, *Air*

Biography CHI/NYC. '70s jazz drummer active in free music. Interesting player. Extensive avant-garde discography includes Arthur Blythe, David Murray, Marion Brown.

Album Title	Name of Artist	Label w Number	Date Recorded	Format	Country
The Chase	Dexter Gordon	Prestige 10010	7/26/70	LP	US
Open Air Suit	Air	Novus/Arista AN 3002	2/21/78	LP	US
Montreux Suisse Air	Air	Novus/Arista AN 3008	7/22/78	LP	US

Name McCurdy, Roy   **Birth Date** 11/28/36

Birthplace Rochester, NY   **Reference** Grove / Feather ('60s and '70s)

Played with Sonny Rollins, Benny Golson, Julian Adderley, Betty Carter

Biography NYC/LA. '60s with artists listed. Exciting, swinging modern drummer. In some ways his time concept is similar to that of Louis Hayes (who also played with Cannonball)—forward moving momentum. Exciting solos.

Album Title	Name of Artist	Label w Number	Date Recorded	Format	Country
*All the Things You Are	Sonny Rollins	RCA 2179-2-RB	7/15/63	CD	US
*Now 's the Time	Sonny Rollins	RCA R25-5-1011	1/24/64	CD	JA
Mercy, Mercy, Mercy	Julian Adderley	Capitol TOCJ - 5323	7/1/66	CD	JA
Cannonball in Japan	Julian Adderley	Capitol B21Y 93560	8/26/66	CD	US

Drummer Discography

Name Mills, Jackie   **Birth Date** 3/11/22

Birthplace New York, NY   **Reference** Grove / Feather (New)

Played with Charlie Barnet, Benny Goodman, Boyd Raeburn, Harry James, Wardell Gray, Sonny Criss

Biography LA. Late '40s - '50s popular bop drummer with substantial discography. Big bands/small groups.

Album Title	Name of Artist	Label w Number	Date Recorded	Format	Country
*Just Jazz	Wardell Gray	GNP KICJ 116/7	2/1/47	2 CDs	JA
*Dodo's Bounce	Dodo Marmarosa	Fresh Sounds 1019	12/3/47	CD	SWI
*Weird Lullaby	Babs Gonsales	Capitol CDP7 81161	4/22/47	CD	US
California Boppin'	Sonny Criss	Fresh Sounds 156	4/29/47	CD	SWI

Name Moffett, Charles   **Birth Date** 9/11/29

Birthplace Fort Worth, TX   **Reference** Grove

Played with Ornette Coleman, Sonny Rollins, Carla Bley

Biography NYC. '60s Original stylist—avant-garde—Ornette Coleman 1962 - '65. Trumpet player.

Album Title	Name of Artist	Label w Number	Date Recorded	Format	Country
Four for Trane	Archie Shepp	Impulse 71	1964	LP	US
O.C. 4 at Golden Circle vol.1	OrnetteColeman	Blue Note B21Y 84224	12/3/65	CD	US
O.C. 4 at Golden Circle vol.2	OrnetteColeman	Blue Note B21Y 84225	12/4/65	CD	US
The Gift	Charles Moffet	Savoy 12194	1969	LP	US

Name Moore, Eddie   **Birth Date** 9/14/40   5/21/91

Birthplace San Francisco, CA   **Reference** Grove

Played with Montgomery brothers, Dexter Gordon, Sonny Rollins, Dewey Redman, Woody Shaw

Biography SF. '60s Montgomery brothers, Dexter Gordon; '70s NYC Stanley Turrentine, Sonny Rollins, Dewey Redman, Woody Shaw; '80s - '91 SF Bobby Hutcherson.

Album Title	Name of Artist	Label w Number	Date Recorded	Format	Country
The Ear of the Behearer	Dewey Redman	Impulse AS 9250	6/8/73	LP	US
Nucleus	Sonny Rollins	Milestone OJCCD 620	9/5/75	CD	US

Name Morell, Marty   **Birth Date** 2/15/44

Birthplace New York, NY   **Reference** Grove / Feather ('70s)

Played with Steve Kuhn, Zoot Sims, Al Cohn, Bill Evans, Jeremy Steig

Biography NYC/CAN. Late '60s - early '70s Bill Evans 1968 - '75. Original brush styles. Assertive, sensitive accompanist—strong soloist. Pianist/percussionist. Currently lves in Toronto—active studio percussionist.

Album Title	Name of Artist	Label w Number	Date Recorded	Format	Country
*October Suite	Steve Kuhn	Impulse MVCI23035	10/14/66	CD	JA
*The Tokyo Concert	Bill Evans	Fantasy OJCCD-345-2	1/20/73	CD	US
*Since We Met	Bill Evans	Fantasy OJCCD-622-2	1/11/74	CD	US
*Re: Person I Knew	Bill Evans	Fantasy OJCCD-749-2	1/11/74	CD	US

Drummer Discography

Name Morello, Joe   **Birth Date** 7/17/28

Birthplace Springfield MA.   **Reference** Grove / Feather (All)

Played with Marion McPartland, Stan Kenton, Tal Farlow, Phil Woods, Dave Brubeck

Biography NYC.'50s Eddie Bert, Phil Woods; '60s DaveBrubeck (odd metered recordings,"Take Five"etc.) virtuosic left hand techniques —solos. Conservative style. One of first drum set clinicians. Teacher/author of several drum books, including one of the first to deal with odd meters.

Album Title	Name of Artist	Label w Number	Date Recorded	Format	Country
Gil Melle 10" LPs on 12"	Gil Melle	Blue Note K18P9275	1/31/53	LP	JA
The Tal Farlow Album	Tal Farlow	Verve MGV 8138	4/11/54	LP	US
The Return of Art Pepper	Art Pepper	Blue Note CDP746863	1/3/57	CD	US
It's About Time	Joe Morello	RCA LPM 2486	9/1/61	LP	US

Name Morton, Jeff   **Birth Date**

Birthplace   **Reference**

Played with Lennie Tristano, Lee Konitz, Ted Brown, Warne Marsh

Biography NYC. Late '40s - '50s Tristano groups. Steady time, excellent accompanist—strong soloist.

Album Title	Name of Artist	Label w Number	Date Recorded	Format	Country
*Subconscious Lee	Lee Konitz	Prestige OJCCD-186-2	9/27/49	CD	US
Konitz	Lee Konitz	Black Lion 760922	8/6/54	CD	GER
Tristano	Lennie Tristano	Atlan. Rhino R2 71595	6/11/55	CD	JA
*Free Wheeling	Ted Brown	Vanguard KI JJ-2066	11/26/56	LP	JA

Name Mosca, Ray   **Birth Date**

Birthplace   **Reference**

Played with George Shearing, Billy Taylor, Carmen Leggio, Hal McKusick

Biography NYC. Late '50 - early '60s versatile, mainstream artists, steady time, nice brushes—popular with pianists: Taylor, Shearing; '70s - '90s active in NYC area.

Album Title	Name of Artist	Label w Number	Date Recorded	Format	Country
George Shearing Quintet	George Shearing	Capitol (S)T1082	3/1/58	LP	US
Billy Uptown	Billy Taylor	Riverside RLP12 319	2/4/60	LP	US
Interlude	Billy Taylor	Moodsville MVLP6	1/3/61	LP	US
The Carmen Leggio group	Carmen Leggio	Jazz Unlimited1000	2/1/61	LP	US

Name Moses, Bob   **Birth Date** 1/28/48

Birthplace NY, NY   **Reference** Grove / Feather ('70s)

Played with Roland Kirk, Dave Liebman, Gary Burton

Biography NYC/BOS '60s Gary Burton; '70s Jack DeJohnette's *Compost*; '80s-'90s leader of own groups—recordings. Exciting, original drummer, influenced by '60s rock styles. Currently on faculty—New England Conservatory. Composer. Author: innovative book *Drum Wisdom*.

Album Title	Name of Artist	Label w Number	Date Recorded	Format	Country
*Lofty Fake Anagram	Gary Burton	RCA LSP 3901	8/15/67	LP	US
Guitar Workshop	Jim Hall	MPS 1514ST	11/5/67	LP	GER
G. Burton Quartet in Concert	Gary Burton	RCA LSP 3985	2/23/68	LP	US
Last Year's Waltz	Steve Kuhn	ECM-1-1213	4/1/81	LP	GER

Drummer Discography

Name Moses, J.C.			**Birth Date** 10/18/36 c. 1977		
Birthplace Pittsburgh, PA.			**Reference** Grove		

Played with Eric Dolphy, Andrew Hill, Clifford Jordan, Kenny Dorham, Bud Powell

Biography John Curtis. NYC. '60s loose, original—exciting soloist with some similarity to Elvin Jones. Bud Powell's drummer (last records).'63 - '64 member avant-garde band *NY Contemporary Five*.

Album Title	Name of Artist	Label w Number	Date Recorded	Format	Country
*Bearcat	Clifford Jordan	Jazzland OJCCD-494-2	12/28/61	CD	US
*Matador	Kenny Dorham	Blue Note CDP7 84460	4/15/62	CD	US
*Vintage Dolphy	Eric Dolphy	GM 3005CD	4/18/63	CD	US
*Ups and Downs	Bud Powell	Mainstream CD724	1964/5	CD	UK

Name Motian, Paul			**Birth Date** 3/25/31		
Birthplace Philadelphia, PA.			**Reference** Grove / Feather (All)		

Played with Lennie Tristano, Bill Evans, Paul Bley, Keith Jarrett, ZootSims, Al Cohn, Stan Getz

Biography NYC. '50s Gil Evans, George Russell; '60s Bley, Evans, Jarrett; '70s composer, leader of own groups—active in '90s. Large, important discography. Versatile, crossover drummer: modern—avant-garde—contemporary styles. Subtle, yet strong. Recommended Evans OJCDs 140, 210.

Album Title	Name of Artist	Label w Number	Date Recorded	Format	Country
*Portrait in Jazz	Bill Evans	RiversideOJCCD-088-2	12/28/59	CD	US
*Jazz is a Kick	Bob Brookmeyer	Mercury SR 60600	6/1/60	LP/CD	US/JA
*Explorations	Bill Evans	RiversideOJCCD-037-2	2/2/61	CD	US
*Turning Point	Paul Bley	Improvising Artists 841	3/9/64	CD	GER

Name Mouzon, Alphonse			**Birth Date** 11/21/48		
Birthplace Charleston, SC			**Reference** Grove / Feather (New)		

Played with Weather Report, Gil Evans, McCoy Tyner, Herbie Hancock, George Benson,

Biography NYC. '70s with artists listed—powerful, exciting jazz/fusion stylist. Records/leads own bands.

Album Title	Name of Artist	Label w Number	Date Recorded	Format	Country
Weather Report	Weather Report	Columbia CK 48824	1971	CD	US
Blues In Orbit	Gil Evans	Enja ENJ-79611-2	1971	CD	US
Sahara	McCoy Tyner	Milestone OJCCD-311	1972	CD	US
Song for the New World	McCoy Tyner	Milestone OJCCD-618	4/1/73	CD	US

Name Muhammad, Idris			**Birth Date** 11/13/39		
Birthplace New Orleans, LA			**Reference** Grove / Feather ('70s)		

Played with Lou Donaldson, Cedar Walton, Don Patton, Donald Byrd, Gene Ammons

Biography Leo Morris. NYC. Late '60 - '70s versatile drummer with a substantial discography—including jazz, funk, soul, and pop recordings. '80s - '90s active in US/Europe.

Album Title	Name of Artist	Label w Number	Date Recorded	Format	Country
*Fancy Free	Donald Byrd	BN CDP 0777 7 89796	6/6/69	CD	US
Turn it On	Sonny Stitt	Prestige PR10012	1/4/71	LP	US
You Talk that Talk	Gene Ammons	Prestige 10019	2/8/71	LP	US
NYC Underground	Johnny Griffin	Galaxy GXY-5132	7/6/79	LP	US

Drummer Discography

Name Murray, Sunny   **Birth Date** 9/21/37

Birthplace Idabel, OK   **Reference** Grove / Feather ('70s)

Played with Albert Ayler, Cecil Taylor, John Coltrane, Archie Shepp

Biography James. NYC. '60s leader of avant-garde styles; '63 John Coltrane; '66 - '90s leads own groups; recorded with Cecil Taylor *Live at Cafe Monmarte.* Aggressive, colorful, ametric "free"drumming. Creates a textural drum sound environment: ESP 1032. Recent years—living in Europe.

Album Title	Name of Artist	Label w Number	Date Recorded	Format	Country
Spiritual Unity	Albert Ayler	ESP 1002	7/10/64	CD	GER
NY Eye and Ear Control	Albert Ayler	ESP 1016	7/17/64	CD	GER
Bells	Albert Ayler	ESP 1010	5/1/65	CD	GER
*Sunny Murray Quintet	Sunny Murray	ESP 1032	1966	CD	GER

Name Nicholson, Ed   **Birth Date**

Birthplace   **Reference**

Played with Dexter Gordon, Tony Scott, Rubberlegs Williams, Miles Davis

Biography NYC. Late '40s early modern drummer who played, recorded with some of the first modernists.

Album Title	Name of Artist	Label w Number	Date Recorded	Format	Country
First Miles	Miles Davis	Savoy SV-0159	4/24/45	CD	JA
*Dexter Rides Again	Dexter Gordon	Savoy SV-0120	10/30/45	CD	JA
Bebop Revisited vol.2	Tony Scott	Xanadu 124	3/6/46	LP	US

Name Noren, Jack   **Birth Date** 10/19/29

Birthplace Chicago, IL   **Reference** Feather (New)

Played with Stan Getz, Gene Ammons, Charlie Parker, Clifford Brown

Biography Sweden. '50s voted most popular modern jazz drummer in Sweden. Substantial discography. Returned to Chicago in late '50s. Sometimes used small mounted bongo as tom-tom alternate.

Album Title	Name of Artist	Label w Number	Date Recorded	Format	Country
Arne Domnerus (out of print)	Arne Domnerus	Savoy MG 9032	8/10/49	LP	US
*Bebop Revisited vol. 1	Charlie Parker	Xanadu FDC 5174	11/22/50	CD	FR
Americans in Europe	Stan Getz	Metronome JM 2102	2/23/51	LP	SWE
*Clifford Brown Memorial	Clifford Brown	Prestige OJCCD 017-2	6/11/53	CD	US

Name Parker, Paul   **Birth Date**

Birthplace   **Reference**

Played with Wes Montgomery, Melvin Rhyne, Freddie Hubbard

Biography Indianapolis. Late '50s - early '60s Wes Montgomery trio—*Pacific Jazz* and *Riverside*.

Album Title	Name of Artist	Label w Number	Date Recorded	Format	Country
*Beginnings	Wes Montgomery	Blue Note LA531- H2	12/30/57	LP	US
*Guitar on the Go	Wes Montgomery	RiversideOJCCD-489-2	11/27/63	CD / CDbox	US
*Wes Montgomery Trio	Wes Montgomery	RiversideOJCCD-034-2	11/27/63	CD / CDbox	US

Drummer Discography

Name Perkins, Walter   **Birth Date** 2/10/32

Birthplace Chicago, IL   **Reference** Grove / Feather ('60s)

Played with Ahmad Jamal, Charles Mingus, Sonny Rollins, Gene Ammons, Jacki Byard, Art Farmer

Biography CHI/NYC. '50s formed MJT plus 3 (CHI); late '50s NY Rollins, Ammons; '50s - '60s large, important discography. Trademark—hand dampens/changes drum or cymbal sound while other hand strikes: "My Little Suede Shoes" *Interaction*. Important, versatile, swinging drummer.

Album Title	Name of Artist	Label w Number	Date Recorded	Format	Country
Love Walked In	Wes Montgomery	Jazzland JLP 55	10/9/61	LP / CD Box	US
*Pike's Peak	Dave Pike	Sony Epic 258P5105	11/1/61	CD	JA
*Interaction	Art Farmer	Atlantic AMCY1015	7/25/63	CD	JA
*Art Farmer live at Half Note	Art Farmer	Atlantic 7 00666-2	12/6/63	CD	US

Name Perry, Charles   **Birth Date**

Birthplace   **Reference**

Played with Stan Getz, Kai Winding, Al Haig, Jimmy Raney, George Wallington

Biography NYC. Late '40s - '50s active modern jazz drummer. Author of drum set instruction books including (with Jack DeJohnette) *The Art of Modern Jazz Drumming* Hal Leonard. .

Album Title	Name of Artist	Label w Number	Date Recorded	Format	Country
*Light Gray	Wardell Gray	Cool 'N Blue CD 116	1949	CD	SWI
A Look at Yesterday	Stan Getz	Mainstream 722	10/1/48	CD	UK
Opus DeBop	Stan Getz	Savoy SJL 1105	5/5/49	LP	US
*George Wallington Trio	George Wallington	Savoy SV-0136	5/9/49	CD	JA

Name Persip, Charlie   **Birth Date** 7/26/29

Birthplace Morristown, NJ   **Reference** Grove / Feather (New and '70s)

Played with Tadd Dameron, Dizzy Gillespie, Donald Byrd, Hank Mobley, Gil Evans, Billy Eckstine

Biography NYC. '50s - '60s important big band drummer: Dizzy Gillespie, Gil Evans—large, important discography—also many classic small group records. Teacher/Jazz mobile. Solid, swinging time. Own records: *Superband*; *Soul Note, Natasha*. Recommended: *Dizzy Atmosphere* OJCCD-1762.

Album Title	Name of Artist	Label w Number	Date Recorded	Format	Country
*Dizzy Atmosphere	Lee Morgan	Specialty OJCCD-1762	2/18/57	CD	US
*Dizzy Gillespie at Newport	Dizzy Gillespie	Verve 314 513 754-2	7/6/57	CD	US
*Duets	Dizzy Gillespie	Verve 835 253-2	12/11/57	CD	US
*Thirty Years of Jazz (1 title)	Gil Evans/Various	Impulse GRD2-101	11/18/60	2 CDs	US

Name Petties, Leon   **Birth Date**

Birthplace   **Reference**

Played with Harold Land, Red Mitchell, Carmell Jones

Biography LA. Discography indicates activity late '40s - early '60s. Savoy LP 2215 is currently out of print.

Album Title	Name of Artist	Label w Number	Date Recorded	Format	Country
Black California (anthology)	Harold Land	Savoy SJL 2215	4/15/49	2 LPs	US
Hear Ye!, Hear Ye!	Red Mitchell	Atlantic 1376-2	10/1/60	CD	US
The Remarkarble C. Jones	Carmell Jones	Pacific Jazz LP29	6/1/61	LP	US

Drummer Discography

Name Porter, Roy **Birth Date** 7/30/23

Birthplace Walsenburg, CO **Reference** Grove

Played with Charlie Parker, Howard McGhee, Dexter Gordon

Biography LA. '40s recorded with Charlie Parker in California on *Dial* . Led own groups including a big band which recorded 4 tracks for Savoy anthology *Black California* SJL 2215 (currently out of print).

Album Title	Name of Artist	Label w Number	Date Recorded	Format	Country
*Bird on Dial (complete)	Charlie Parker	Stash STCD567/8/9/10	3/28/46	4 CD Box	US
*Trumpet at Tempo	Howard McGhee	Spotlite SPJ 131	7/29/46	LP	UK
*Steady with Teddy	Teddy Edwards	Cool 'N Blue CD 115	12/4/47	CD	SWI
*Complete Dean Benedetti	Charlie Parker	Mosaic MD7-129	3/12/47	7 CD Box	US

Name Pratt, Jimmy **Birth Date**

Birthplace **Reference**

Played with Charlie Parker, Zoot Sims, Herb Geller, Oscar Pettiford

Biography LA. Late '40s - '50s recorded with modernists; late '50s - 60s recorded in Europe.

Album Title	Name of Artist	Label w Number	Date Recorded	Format	Country
*Bird on Dial (complete)	Charlie Parker	Stash STCD567/8/9/10	2/1/47	4 CD Box	US
*Zootcase	Zoot Sims	Prestige 24061	1/16/54	2 LPs	US
The Legendary O.Pettiford	Oscar Pettiford	Black Lion 30185	1/10/59	LP	GER
O.P. and Hans Kollerquintet	Oscar Pettiford	Saba 15024ST	2/19/59	LP	GER

Name Queen, Alvin **Birth Date** 8/16/50

Birthplace New York, NY **Reference** Grove

Played with George Benson, Stanley Turrentine, Charles Tolliver, Jr. Mance, Kenny Drew

Biography NYC/Europe 1979 moved to Europe, where he lives currently. Strong, swinging player.

Album Title	Name of Artist	Label w Number	Date Recorded	Format	Country
Pannonica	Horace Paran	Enja 4076	2/11/81	LP	GER
Soul Connection	John Patton	Nilva NQ 3406	6/7/83	LP	US
Impressions	Kenny Drew	Alpha 32R2-14	8/1/88	CD	JA
Expressions	Kenny Drew	Alpha ALCR-65	5/7/90	CD	JA

Name Rae, John **Birth Date** 8/11/34   8/1/93

Birthplace Boston, MA **Reference** Grove / Feather (All)

Played with George Shearing, Bola Sete, Cal Tjader, Vince Guaraldi, Stan Getz, Gary McFarland

Biography Pompeo SF. Drummer, vibraphonist (with Shearing), percussionist. Own record dates (listed). Author: first (and best, to date) jazz drummer's book about Latin patterns: *Latin Guide for Jazz Drummers,* also mallet studies. Plays vibes on Savoy SV-0179, Jake Hanna is the drummer.

Album Title	Name of Artist	Label w Number	Date Recorded	Format	Country
Opus De Jazz vol. 2 (vibes)	John Rae	Savoy SV-0179	12/6/60	CD	JA
John Rae Afro-Jazz Septet	John Rae	United Artists 4042	1961	LP	US
*Big Band Bossa Nova	Stan Getz	Verve 833 535-2	8/27/62	CD	US
Cal Tjader Quartet	Cal Tjader	Verve V(S)8531	1/28/63	LP	US

Drummer Discography

Name Rice, Charlie   **Birth Date**

Birthplace   **Reference**

Played with J.J. Johnson, Howard McGhee, Sonny Stitt, Eddie Davis, Chet Baker, Leo Parker

Biography NYC. '50s - '60s poular bop drummer—loose swing.

Album Title	Name of Artist	Label w Number	Date Recorded	Format	Country
South Pacific Jazz	Howard McGhee	Savoy SV-0219	1952	CD	JA
Stitt and Jaws at Birdland	S.Stitt / Eddie Davis	Blue Note B21Y 97507	1954	CD	US
Let Me Tell You 'Bout it	Leo Parker	Blue Note CDP784087	9/9/61	CD	US
Chet Baker	Chet Baker	Colpix CLP 476	1964	LP	US

Name Rich, Buddy   **Birth Date** *9/30/17   4/2/87

Birthplace New York, NY   **Reference** Grove / Feather (All)

Played with Tommy Dorsey, Artie Shaw, Harry James, Lester Young, Charlie Parker, Bud Powell, JATP

Biography Bernard. NYC. '40s Dorsey, Shaw, James; '50s Young, Parker, Powell; '60s - '87 led own bands. Although best known for swing innovations, recorded with bop masters. Important drummer—huge discog. For more bio., see *Traps, Drum Wonder* Mel Torme. *Feather: 6/30/17.

Album Title	Name of Artist	Label w Number	Date Recorded	Format	Country
*L. Young and Piano Giants	Lester Young	Verve 835 3116-2	12/1/45	CD	US
*Bird and Diz	Charlie Parker	Verve 831133-2	6/6/50	CD	US
*The Genius of Bud Powell	Bud Powell	Verve 827 901 2	7/1/50	CD	US
*Drums Ablaze (broadcasts)	Art Blakey	Alto 721	4/23/60	LP	US

Name Richmond, Danny   **Birth Date** 12/15/35   3/16/88

Birthplace New York, NY   **Reference** Grove / Feather (All)

Played with Charles Mingus, Bud Powell, Chet Baker, Zoot Sims, Herbie Nichols

Biography NYC. Late '50s - '80s large, important discography—favorite drummer of Charles Mingus. Swings. Original, lively, and unpredictable. Also led his own recordings, and *Mingus Dynasty*.

Album Title	Name of Artist	Label w Number	Date Recorded	Format	Country
*Herbie Nichols	Herbie Nichols	Bethlehem BCP-6028	1957	LP	US
*New Tiajuana Moods	Charles Mingus	Bluebird 4644-2- RB	7/18/57	CD	US
*Mingus Ah Um	Charles Mingus	Columbia CK- 40648	5/5/59	CD	US
*The Book Cooks	Booker Ervin/Sims	Bethlehem BCP 6048	6/1/60	LP	US/JA

Name Riel, Alex   **Birth Date** 9/13/40

Birthplace Copenhagen   **Reference** Grove / Feather ('70s)

Played with Dexter Gordon, Kenny Dorham, Ben Webster, Kenny Drew, Jackie McLean

Biography Denmark. '60s - '70s accompanied, recorded with American jazz musicians in Europe.

Album Title	Name of Artist	Label w Number	Date Recorded	Format	Country
Scandaia Skies	Kenny Dorham	SteepleChase 6011	12/5/63	CD	DEN
Short Story	Kenny Dorham	SteepleChase 6010	12/19/63	CD	DEN
Live at Monmartre 1972	Jackie McLean	SteepleChase 1001	8/5/72	CD	DEN
The Source	Dexter Gordon	SteepleChase 1006	7/20/73	CD	DEN

Drummer Discography

Name Riley, Ben   **Birth Date** 7/17/33

Birthplace Savannah, GA   **Reference** Grove / Feather ('60s and '70s)

Played with Thelonious Monk, Randy Weston, Sonny Stitt, Kenny Burrell, Stan Getz, *Sphere*

Biography NYC. '60s popular sideman, recording artist—large, important discography (Monk '64-7); '70s formed group *Sphere* with fellow Monk quartet member, Charlie Rouse, pianist Kenny Baron, and bassist Buster Williams; Currently active in NYC. Solid swing and ensemble flexibility.

Album Title	Name of Artist	Label w Number	Date Recorded	Format	Country
*The Bridge	Sonny Rollins	Bluebird 07863-61061	2/13/62	CD	US
*What's New	Sonny Rollins	Bluebird 07863-52572	4/5/62	CD	US
*It's Monk's Time	Thelonious Monk	Col. Sony 468 405 2	1/29/64	CD	AUS
*Live at the Jazz Workshop	Thelonious Monk	Col. Sony 469183 2	11/4/64	2 CDs	AUS

Name Ritchie, Larry   **Birth Date**

Birthplace   **Reference**

Played with Ray Draper, Freddie Redd, Jackie McLean

Biography NYC. Late '50s - early '60s with artists listed, off-broadway show/recording *The Connection.*

Album Title	Name of Artist	Label w Number	Date Recorded	Format	Country
Fat Jazz	Jackie McLean	Fresh Sounds CD13	11/27/57	CD	SP
R.D.quintet feat. J. Coltrane	Ray Draper	New Jazz LP 8228	12/20/57	LP / CD Box	US
Tuba Jazz	Ray Draper	Fresh Sounds FSR-20	11/1/58	CD	SP
Music from *the Connection*	Freddie Redd	Blue Note BLP4027	2/15/60	LP	US

Name Roach, Max   **Birth Date** 1/10/24

Birthplace New Land, NC   **Reference** Grove / Feather (All)

Played with Benny Carter, Charlie Parker, Dizzy Gillespie, Bud Powell, George Wallington, J.J. Johnson

Biography NYC. See pages 30-34 for a more extensive biography. Discography here represents his early period—from late '40s - mid '50's. All Bird recordings,especially *Savoy*s are recommended. There are some fine recordings by Roach's own groups from mid '50s - '90s, including *M'Boom.*

Album Title	Name of Artist	Label w Number	Date Recorded	Format	Country
*Trio plays: Roost Sessions	Bud Powell	Rouiette B21Y 93902	1/10/47	CD	US
* Bird on Dial (complete)	Charlie Parker	Stash STCD567/8/9/10	10/28/47	4 CD Box	US
*Jazz at Massey Hall: Quintet	Charlie Parker	Debut OJCCD-044-2	5/15/53	CD	US
* Brownie: Complete EmArcy	Clifford Brown/M.R.	EmArcy 838 306-2	8/2/54	10 CD Box	US

Name Roker, Mickey   **Birth Date** 9/3/32

Birthplace Miami, FL   **Reference** Grove / Feather ('60s and '70s)

Played with Gigi Gryce, Ray Bryant, Art Farmer, Dizzy Gillespie, Sonny Rollins, Mit Jackson, Jim Hall

Biography Granville. NYC.'60s - '70s popular accompanist with large, important discography; '80s - '90s—continues career. Steady, basic, swinging style. Versatile: small group— and outstanding big band drummer—*Now Hear This.* Uses interesting broken hi-hat figures—*Speak Like a Child.*

Album Title	Name of Artist	Label w Number	Date Recorded	Format	Country
*The Standard Sonny Rollins	Sonny Rollins	RCA R25J-1012	7/2/62	CD	JA
*Sonny Rollins on Impulse	Sonny Rollins	Impulse MCAD 5655	7/8/65	CD	US
*Speak Like a Child	Herbie Hancock	Blue Note B21Y 46136	3/9/68	CD	US
*Now Hear This	Duke Pearson	Blue Note BLP 4303	12/2/68	LP	US

Drummer Discography

Name Romano, Aldo   **Birth Date** 1/16/41

Birthplace Belluno, Italy   **Reference** Grove

Played with Steve Kuhn, Steve Swallow, Barney Wilen, Jackie McLean

Biography Europe. Late '60s exciting record with Kuhn, somewhat reminiscent of Pete La Roca. Loose, uninhibited, original style influenced by Elvin Jones; '70s - '90s leads own groups, recordings in Europe.

Album Title	Name of Artist	Label w Number	Date Recorded	Format	Country
*Childhood is Forever	Steve Kuhn	BYG 529 136	10/13/69	LP	GER
Divieto DeSanctification	Aldo Romano	Horo 07	1977	LP	IT
Alma Latina	Aldo Romano	Owl 031	1983	LP	FR
Oceans in the Sky	Steve Kuhn	Owl R2 79232	9/20/89	CD	FR

Name Ruggiero, Vincent   **Birth Date** c.1975

Birthplace Elmont, LI-NY   **Reference**

Played with Slide Hampton, Joe Romano, Sal Nistico, Chuck Mangione, James Brown

Biography NYC. Late '50s - early '60s active in NYC— Slide Hampton; '60s Rochester NY— Chuck Mangione.Became teacher— authentic modern drumming; '70s died, Long Island. Legendary for collaborations with PJ Jones, transcribing his drumming. Strong swinging time, and solos.

Album Title	Name of Artist	Label w Number	Date Recorded	Format	Country
Spring Fever	Chuck Mangione	RiversideOJCCD-767-2	11/28/61	CD	US
Explosion	Slide Hampton	Atlantic SD 1396	7/26/62	LP	US
*Comin' on Up	Sal Nistico	Riverside RLP 457	10/17/62	LP	US
*Exodus	Slide Hampton	Philips BL 77915	11/14/62	LP	US

Name Schiopffe, William   **Birth Date**

Birthplace   **Reference**

Played with Stan Getz, Bud Powell, Arne Domnerus

Biography Sweden. Late '50s - early '60s Scandinavian drummer with a substantial discography in Europe.

Album Title	Name of Artist	Label w Number	Date Recorded	Format	Country
Stockholm Sessions'58	Stan Getz	DIW-137/138	9/16/58	2 CDs	JA
Scandinavian Days	Stan Getz	Fresh Sounds1009	3/1/59	CD	SWI
Stan Getz at Large vol. 1	Stan Getz	Jazz Unlimited 2001	1960	CD	US
*Bouncing with Bud	Bud Powell	Storyville 4113	4/26/62	CD	US

Name Segal, Jerry   **Birth Date** 2/16/31

Birthplace Philadelphia, PA   **Reference** Grove / Feather (New)

Played with Teddy Charles, Benny Green, Stan Getz, Charles Mingus, Mose Allison

Biography Gerald. NYC. '50s swinging, active bop drummer with a substantial discograpy.

Album Title	Name of Artist	Label w Number	Date Recorded	Format	Country
Evolution	Teddy Charles	Prestige OJCCD-1731	1/6/55	CD	US
C.Fuller with Hampton Hawes	Curtis Fuller	Prestige PRLP16-5	5/18/57	LP	US
*The 45 Session	Benny Green	Blue Note 61020	11/23/58	LP	JA
Mose Allison	Mose Allison	Columbia CL1444	12/21/59	LP	US

Drummer Discography

Name Shaughnessy, Ed   **Birth Date** 1/29/29

Birthplace Jersey City, NJ   **Reference** Grove / Feather (All)

Played with Charlie Ventura, Charlie Parker, Charles Mingus, Teddy Charles, Booker Little, Gary McFarland

Biography NYC/LA. Late '40s used 2 bass drums with Ventura's *Bop for the People* band; '50s to early '60s active jazz recording Mingus, Charles, Little ; 60s NY studios; '70s/'80s LA "Tonight show".

Album Title	Name of Artist	Label w Number	Date Recorded	Format	Country
*A CharlieVentura Concert	Charlie Ventura	Decca MCAD 42330	5/9/49	CD	US
*The Jazz Guitarist	Chuck Wayne	Savoy SV-0189	4/13/53	CD	JA
*The Gary McFarland Orch.	Gary McFarland	Verve MGV 8518	1/24/63	LP	US
*Groovy Sound of Music	Gary Burton	RCA LPM 3360	12/22/64	LP	US

Name Smith, Charlie   **Birth Date** 4/15/27   1/15/66

Birthplace New York, NY   **Reference** Grove / Feather (New and '60s)

Played with Ella Fitzgerald, Charlie Parker, Dizzy Gillespie, Erroll Garner, Billy Taylor

Biography NYC. '50s drummer on the only known film of Charlie Parker performance — film clip of a show with Dizzy '52 (listed). The video clearly demonstrates Smith's early '50s bop drumming style.

Album Title	Name of Artist	Label w Number	Date Recorded	Format	Country
Oscar Pettiford Discoveries	Oscar Pettiford	Savoy SJL 1172	2/21/52	LP	US
*Celebrating Bird	Charlie Parker	Sony JO509 (VHS)	4/1/52	Video Tape	US
Milt Jackson and the All Stars	Milt Jackson	Vogue 655 005	3/7/54	CD	FR

Name Smith, Jimmy   **Birth Date** 1/27/38

Birthplace Newark, NJ   **Reference** Grove / Feather ('70s)

Played with Buddy DeFranco, Larry Young, Erroll Garner

Biography NYC. '60s - '70s popular jazz/blues recording artist.

Album Title	Name of Artist	Label w Number	Date Recorded	Format	Country
Testifying	Larry Young	Prestige OJCCD-1793	8/2/60	CD	US
Forrest Fire	Jimmy Forrest	Prestige OJCCD-199-2	8/9/60	CD	US
Ellington is Forever	Kenny Burrell	Fantasy 79005	2/4/75	CD	US
Just Friends	Zoot Sims	Pablo OJCCD-499-2	12/18/78	CD	US

Name Smith, Warren   **Birth Date** 5/4/32

Birthplace Chicago, IL   **Reference** Grove / Feather ('70s)

Played with Sam Rivers, Nat Cole, Gil Evans, George Russell, Charles Mingus, Elvin Jones, Max Roach

Biography NYC. '70s - '90s important percussionist/drummer—large percussion discography. Member of *M'Boom* percussion ensemble. Associate professor Sunny Purchase, NY. For two additional titles—Smith's own *Strata-East* LPs—see Clay, Omar (p. 61).

Album Title	Name of Artist	Label w Number	Date Recorded	Format	Country
*Let My Children Hear Music	Charles Mingus	Columbia CK - 48910	9/23/71	CD	US
*The Prime Element	Elvin Jones	Blue Note LA 506 H2	7/24/73	2 LPs	US
*Collage (percussion)	M'BoomMax Roach	Soul Note SN 1059	1984	CD	IT
M'Boom Live at S.O.B.'s (p.)	M'BoomMax Roach	BlueMoonMRR279182	1/9/92	CD	US

Drummer Discography

Name Stabulas, Nick   **Birth Date** 12/18/29   2/6/73

Birthplace New York, NY   **Reference** Grove / Feather (New)

Played with Phil Woods, George Wallington, Gil Evans, Zoot Sims

Biography NYC. '50s popular, swinging bop drummer with a substantial discography. Influenced by Arthur Taylor and Philly Joe Jones.

Album Title	Name of Artist	Label w Number	Date Recorded	Format	Country
Woodlore	Phil Woods	Prestige OJCCD-052-2	12/25/55	CD	US
*The New York Scene	George Wallington	New Jazz OJCCD-1805	3/1/57	CD	US
*Gil Evans Plus Ten	Gil Evans	Prestige OJCCD-346-2	9/6/57	CD	US
Jazz at Hotchkiss	George Wallington	Savoy SV-0119	11/14/57	CD	JA

Name Stewart, Teddy   **Birth Date**

Birthplace   **Reference**

Played with Dizzy Gillespie, Gene Ammons, Sonny Stitt

Biography NYC. Late '40s - early '50s Dizzy Gillespie's big band—popular bop drummer—strong, swinging time.

Album Title	Name of Artist	Label w Number	Date Recorded	Format	Country
*Legendary Big Band	Dizzy Gillespie	Vogue 651600025	7/26/48	CD	FR
*From Swing to Bebop	Dizzy Gillespie	RCA RA 96-100	12/29/48	4 LP Box	JA
*First Sessions vol. 2	Sonny Stitt	Prestige 24115	1/31/51	CD	US
*Gene Ammons story (78era)	Gene Ammons	Prestige 24058	6/29/51	CD	US

Name Stoller, Alvin   **Birth Date** 10/7/25   10/19/92

Birthplace New York, NY   **Reference** Grove / Feather (New)

Played with Harry James, Claude Thornhill, George Auld,Coleman Hawkins, Oscar Peterson,

Biography LA. Late '40s - '50s big band—small group studio recording, Norman Granz *Mercury, Clef.*

Album Title	Name of Artist	Label w Number	Date Recorded	Format	Country
*Early Bebop	Neal Hefti	Mercury 830 922-2	12/18/46	CD	JA
Oscar Peterson Quartet	Oscar Peterson	Verve MGV 8127	12/1/51	LP	US
Ray Brown Big Band	Ray Brown	Verve MGV 8022	11/1/56	LP	US
C. Hawkins and Ben Webster	Coleman Hawkins	Verve 833 296-2	10/16/57	CD	US

Name Tate, Grady   **Birth Date** 1/14/32

Birthplace Durham, NC   **Reference** Grove / Feather ('60s and '70s)

Played with Donald Byrd, Quincy Jones, Kenny Burrell,Stan Getz, Miles Davis

Biography NYC. '60s popular jazz studio recording artist. Large discography, especially big band sessions. Recorded own albums as a singer.

Album Title	Name of Artist	Label w Number	Date Recorded	Format	Country
More Blues & Abstract Truth	Oliver Nelson	Impulse A (S)9101	11/10/64	LP	US
The Dynamic Duo	Jimmy Smith	Verve 821577-2	9/28/66	CD	US
*Sweet Rain	Stan Getz	Verve 815054-2	3/3/67	CD	US
Zoot and Gershwin brothers	Zoot Sims	Pablo OJCCD-444-2	6/6/75	CD	US

Drummer Discography

Name Taylor, Arthur   **Birth Date** 4/6/29

Birthplace New York, NY   **Reference** Grove / Feather (New and '60s)

Played with Miles Davis, Charlie Parker, Thelonious Monk, Bud Powell, John Coltrane

Biography NYC.'50s' - 60s very important modern drummer with a large, vital discography. Currently remains active, leads own group, *Taylor's Wailers*. His strong swing—cymbal ride, and hi-hat—influenced many drummers. Author: *Note and Tones: Musician to Musician interviews* DaCapo.

Album Title	Name of Artist	Label w Number	Date Recorded	Format	Country
*Amazing Bud Powell vol.2	Bud Powell	Blue Note B21Y 81504	8/14/53	CD	US
*C. Parker Plays Cole Porter	Charlie Parker	Verve MGV 8001	12/10/54	LP/ CD Box	US
*Quintet/Sextet	Miles Davis	Prestige OJCCD-012-2	8/5/55	CD/ CD Box	US
*Giant Steps	John Coltrane	Atlantic 1311-2	5/4/59	CD	US

Name Thigpen, Ed   **Birth Date** 12/28/30

Birthplace Chicago, IL   **Reference** Grove / Feather (All)

Played with Bud Powell, Billy Taylor, John Coltrane, Oscar Peterson, Sonny Stitt, Kenny Drew, Art Farmer

Biography NYC/Denmark. mid '50s - late '60s large, important discography with artists listed. Moved to Copenhagen in 1972, where he still resides. Renown educator. Author: drum set books, including *The Sound of Brushes*. Polished, swinging style—popular with great pianists listed.

Album Title	Name of Artist	Label w Number	Date Recorded	Format	Country
*Winner's Circle (Bethlehem)	John Coltrane	BR-5030/BCP-6066	10/57	CD	JA
*Sonny Stitt Sits In with O.P.	Oscar Peterson	Verve 849 396-2	5/18/59	CD	US
*O. P. plays the Cole Porter..	Oscar Peterson	Verve 821 987-2	7/21/59	CD	US
*Manhattan	Art Farmer	Soul Note 121026-2	11/29/81	CD	IT

Name Thomas, Bobby   **Birth Date**

Birthplace NJ   **Reference**

Played with Billy Taylor, Wes Montgomery, Richard Williams, Art Farmer, Gigi Gryce

Biography NYC. '60s popuar, swinging NYC modern drummer/percussionist. Oddly, his drumming discography is small.

Album Title	Name of Artist	Label w Number	Date Recorded	Format	Country
New Horn in Town	Richard Williams	Candid 9003	9/27/60	CD	GER
*Groove Yard	Wes Montgomery	Riverside12-362	1/3/61	LP / CD Box	US
*Reminiscin'	Gigi Gryce	Mercury MG 20628	1/10/61	LP	US
*The Many Faces of Art	Art Farmer	Scepter 521	1964	LP	US

Name Thompson, Chuck   **Birth Date** 6/4/26

Birthplace New York, NY   **Reference** Grove

Played with Charlie Parker, Miles Davis, Wardell Gray, Hampton Hawes, Dexter Gordon, Howard McGhee

Biography LA. Late '40s - '50s substantial discography with important jazz artists listed.

Album Title	Name of Artist	Label w Number	Date Recorded	Format	Country
*Yardbird in Lotus Land	Charlie Parker	Spotlite SPJ 123	3/1/46	LP	UK
*Dexter's Mood	Dexter Gordon	Cool 'N Blue CD114	6/12/47	CD	SWI
*Wardell Gray Memorial vol. 2	Wardell Gray	Prestige OJCCD-051-2	8/27/50	CD	US
H.Hawes,The Trio (vols. 1-3)	Hampton Hawes	OJCCDs316,318,421	11/12/55	CDs (3)	US

Drummer Discography

Name Timer, Joe   **Birth Date** 3/21/23

Birthplace Alexandria,VA   **Reference** Feather (New)

Played with Lennie Tristano, Elliot Lawrence, Charlie Parker, Dizzy Gillespie

Biography DC. '50s leader DC. big band (with Willis Conover)—recorded live concerts with Bird, and Dizzy.

Album Title	Name of Artist	Label w Number	Date Recorded	Format	Country
*One Night in Washington	Charlie Parker	Electra Musician 60019	2/22/53	LP	US
One Night in Washington	Dizzy Gillespie	Electra Musician 60300	3/13/55	LP	US

Name Tough, Dave   **Birth Date** 4/26/07   12/9/48

Birthplace Oak Park, IL   **Reference** Grove / Feather (New)

Played with Woody Herman, Benny Goodman, Charlie Ventura

Biography NYC. Late '30s - '48 important early modern drummer. Original sound, unique sense of time. One of first swing drummers, with Clarke, to play ride cymbal/use irregular b.d. patterns. Writer and satirist. Author: *Paraddidle Studies* (very rare). *Mercury*, listed, has better sound/fewer tiles.

Album Title	Name of Artist	Label w Number	Date Recorded	Format	Country
*Genius of the Electric Guitar	Charlie Christian	Columbia CK- 40846	10/2/39	CD	US
*The Happy Monster	Chubby Jackson	Cool 'N Blue CD 109	10/2/44	CD	SWI
*Small Herd /same as C&B	Chubby Jackson	Mercury 830 968-2	1/10/45	CD	JA
*The Thundering Herds	Woody Herman	Columbia CK44108	2/19/45	CD	US

Name Turner, Milt   **Birth Date**

Birthplace   **Reference**

Played with Ray Charles, David Newman,Teddy Edwards, Phineas Newborn, Joe Gordon, Leroy Vinnegar

Biography LA.Late '50s - early '60s with artists listed. (Recorded David Newman's LP *Fathead—Atlantic* 1304 in NYC, 11/5/58). Known for swinging time.

Album Title	Name of Artist	Label w Number	Date Recorded	Format	Country
Lookin' Good	Joe Gordon	Contemporary OJC174	7/11/61	LP	US
Good Gravy	Teddy Edwards	Contem.OJCCD-661-2	8/23/61	CD	US
Great Jazz Piano	Phineas Newborn	Contem.OJCCD-388-2	9/12/62	CD	US
Leroy Walks Again	Leroy Vinnegar	Contem.OJCCD-454-2	8/1/61	CD	US

Name Viale, Jean Louis   **Birth Date** 1/22/33   5/10/84

Birthplace France   **Reference** Grove / Feather ('60s)

Played with Bobby Jaspar, Clifford Brown, Gigi Gryce, Zoot Sims, Frank Rosolino, Jimmy Raney

Biography Paris. '50s French drummer. Recorded with visiting American jazz musicians in Europe.

Album Title	Name of Artist	Label w Number	Date Recorded	Format	Country
*Clifford Brown big band	Clifford Brown	Prestige OJCCD-359-2	9/28/53	CD	US
Clifford Brown quartet	Clifford Brown	Prestige OJCCD-358-2	9/29/53	CD	US
Zoot Sims & Frank Rosolino	Zoot Sims	Vogue 655622	11/18/53	CD	FR
Jimmy Raney in Paris	Jimmy Raney	Fresh Sounds 089	2/10/54	CD	SP

Drummer Discography

Name Waits, Freddie   **Birth Date** 4/27/43   11/18/89

Birthplace Jackson, MS   **Reference** Grove / Feather ('70s)

Played with Ray Bryant, McCoy Tyner, Curtis Fuller, Freddie Hubbard, Andrew Hill, Hank Mobley

Biography NYC. Late '60s - '70s active with a substantial discography, both as drummer and percussionist; '80s Max Roach's *M'Boom—Collage, Soul Note* CD1059. Lively, forward moving style. Death date listed is approximate.

Album Title	Name of Artist	Label w Number	Date Recorded	Format	Country
*Mustang	Donald Byrd	Blue Note 4238	6/24/66	LP	US
High Blues Pressure	Freddie Hubbard	Atlantic LP 1501	11/13/67	LP	US
Grass Roots	Andrew Hill	Blue Note 84303	1968	LP	US
Expansions	McCoy Tyner	Blue Note 84338	1968	LP	US

Name Walker, Hugh   **Birth Date**

Birthplace   **Reference**

Played with Kenny Dorham, Harold Mabern, John Patton

Biography NYC. Late '60s swinging bop drummer with minimal, but strong discography.

Album Title	Name of Artist	Label w Number	Date Recorded	Format	Country
*Shadow of Your Smile	Kenny Dorham	West Wind 2049	2/25/66	CD	GER
Got a Good Thing Goin'	John Patton	Blue Note BLP4229	4/29/66	LP	US
Straight Up	Harold Vick	RCA LPM 3761	10/3/66	LP	US
Rakin' and Scrapin'	Harold Mabern	Prestige OJC-330	12/23/68	LP	US

Name West, Harold "Doc"   **Birth Date** 8/12/15   5/4/51

Birthplace Wolford, ND   **Reference** Grove / Feather (New)

Played with Hot Lips Page, Charlie Parker, Wardell Gray, Errol Garner

Biography NYC. Mid '40s popular swing/early modern drummer, played at Minton's club (Harlem). Important discography. *Spotlite* LP 129 is mostly piano solos.

Album Title	Name of Artist	Label w Number	Date Recorded	Format	Country
*The Immortal Charlie Parker	Charlie Parker	Savoy SV-0102	9/15/44	CD	JA
*One for Pres	Wardell Gray	Black Lion 60106	11/23/46	CD	GER
*Bird on Dial (complete)	Charlie Parker	Stash STCD567/8/9/10	2/19/47	4 CD Box	US
*Play Piano, Play	Erroll Garner	Spotlite LP 129	2/19/47	LP	UK

Name White, Bobby   **Birth Date** 6/28/26

Birthplace Chicago, IL   **Reference** Grove / Feather (New)

Played with Charlie Barnet, Buddy DeFranco, Art Pepper, Sonny Clark, Jimmy Raney

Biography LA. '50s smooth, swinging drummer—a favorite of Buddy DeFranco. Influenced by Art Blakey.

Album Title	Name of Artist	Label w Number	Date Recorded	Format	Country
*Surf Ride	Art Pepper	Savoy SV-0115	10/8/52	CD	JA
*Sonny Clark Memorial	Sonny Clark	Xanadu BRJ 4552	1/15/54	CD	JA
*Autumn Leaves	Buddy DeFranco	Verve MGV 8183	8/9/54	LP	US
*In a Mellow Mood	Buddy DeFranco	Verve MGV 8169	8/10/54	LP	US

Drummer Discography

Name White, Lenny   **Birth Date** 12/19/49

Birthplace New York, NY   **Reference** Grove / Feather ('70s)

Played with George Russell, Chick Corea, Stan Getz, Joe Henderson, Freddie Hubbard

Biography NYC. '70s with artists listed—loose jazz drummer, adept with both late modern and fusion styles.

Album Title	Name of Artist	Label w Number	Date Recorded	Format	Country
Bitches Brew	Miles Davis	Columbia G2K-40577	8/19/69	2 CDs	US
*Red Clay	Freddie Hubbard	CTI 6007	11/16/70	LP	US
In Pursuit of Blackness	Joe Henderson	Milestone MSP9034	5/12/71	LP	US
*Echos of an Era	Chick Corea	Elektra 60021	1981	LP	US

Name Williams, Jeff   **Birth Date** 7/6/50

Birthplace Mt. Vernon, OH   **Reference**

Played with Dave Leibman, Stan Getz, Don Friedman, John Abercrombie, Art Farmer, Lee Konitz

Biography NYC. '70s Stan Getz, *Lookout Farm*; '80s Jerry Bergonzi, Mick Goodrick, Miroslav Vitous; '90s Joe Lavano, Lee Konitz. Formed, recorded own quintet. Smooth, loose swing—suited for '70s, '80s jazz styles.

Album Title	Name of Artist	Label w Number	Date Recorded	Format	Country
*Lookout Farm	Lookout Farm	ECM 1039	1973	LP	GER
*Eon	Richard Beirach	ECM 1054	11/74	LP	GER
Paul Bley plays Carla Bley	Paul Bley	SteepleChase 31303	1992	CD	DEN
Coalescence	Jeff Williams	SteepleChase 31308	1992	CD	DEN

Name Williams, Leroy   **Birth Date** 2/3/37

Birthplace Chicago, IL   **Reference** Grove / Feather ('70s)

Played with Barry Harris, Sonny Stitt, Jr. Cook, Hank Mobley, Al Cohn, Sonny Rollins

Biography NYC. '70s - '80s loose bop drummer—interesting soloist *Complete quartets with B.H.* Popular in trios/small groups— strong discography. A favorite of Barry Harris.

Album Title	Name of Artist	Label w Number	Date Recorded	Format	Country
*Thinking of Home	Hank Mobley	Blue Note LT 1095	7/31/70	LP	US
*Barry Harris Live	Barry Harris	Xanadu FDC 5155	4/12/76	CD	FR
*Complete quartets with B.H. Al Cohn		Xanadu FDC 5171	12/6/76	CD	FR
*Barry Harris plays B. H.	Barry Harris	Xanadu FDC 5173	1/18/78	CD	FR

Name Williams, Tony   **Birth Date** 12/12/45

Birthplace Chicago, IL   **Reference** Grove / Feather ('60s and '70s)

Played with Miles Davis, Jackie McLean, Herbie Hancock, Freddie Hubbard, Hank Jones

Biography Anthony. NYC. See pages 49-50 for a more extensive biograpy. Discography here represents early (60's) period with Miles Davis. All recordings with Miles are recommended. See page 50 for *Lifetime* recordings. His most recent recordings are on *Blue Note*.

Album Title	Name of Artist	Label w Number	Date Recorded	Format	Country
*Seven Steps to Heaven	Miles Davis	Columbia CK- 48827	5/14/63	CD	US
*The complete concert:1964	Miles Davis	Columbia C2K-48821-2	2/12/64	2 CDs	US
*Nefertiti	Miles Davis	Columbia CK- 44113	6/7/67	CD	US
*Miles in the Sky	Miles Davis	Columbia CK- 48954	1/16/68	CD	US

Drummer Discography

Name Wilson, Shadow   **Birth Date** 9/25/19   7/11/59

Birthplace Yonkers, NY   **Reference** Grove / Feather (New)

Played with Count Basie, Woody Herman, Earl Hines, Thelonious Monk, Sonny Stitt

Biography NYC. Rossiere. '40s -'50s often overlooked, very important modern drummer with large, vital jazz discography—big band swing— small group bop. Subtle hi-hat and ride cymbal styles. Provided superb accompaniment— strong, light swing. His work is on the high level of Clarke's.

Album Title	Name of Artist	Label w Number	Date Recorded	Format	Country
*One O'Clock Jump	Count Basie	Sony 258P 5121	1/6/46	CD	JA
*Johnson's Jazz Quintets	J.J. Johnson	Savoy SV-0151	12/24/47	CD	JA
*Sonny Stitt Plays	Sonny Stitt	Fresh Sounds CD 92	9/1/56	CD	SP
*T. Monk with John Coltrane	Thelonious Monk	Jazzland OJCCD-039-2	7/1/57	CD	US

Name Wise, Arnie   **Birth Date**

Birthplace   **Reference**

Played with Bill Evans, Dave Pike

Biography NYC. Late '60s Bill Evans' drummer—early '66. Nice brushes.

Album Title	Name of Artist	Label w Number	Date Recorded	Format	Country
*Bill Evans at Town Hall	Bill Evans	Verve 83127-2	2/21/66	CD	US
Live at the Village Gate	Dave Pike	Vortex SD 2007	9/28/66	LP	US

Name Woodyard, Sam   **Birth Date** 1/7/25   9/20/88

Birthplace Elizabeth, NJ   **Reference** Grove / Feather (All)

Played with Duke Ellington, Roy Eldridge, Joe Holiday, Paul Gonsalves, John Coltrane

Biography NYC. '50s Duke Ellington's favorite drummer (after Sonny Greer)—with Duke, on and off, from '55 - '66. Strong, loose cymbal time. Trade mark is is a cross stick over the rim of his snare drum, doubling the hi-hat on the backbeats (2 and 4).

Album Title	Name of Artist	Label w Number	Date Recorded	Format	Country
*Ellington at Newport	Duke Ellington	Columbia CK- 40587	7/4/56	CD	US
*D. E. vol.7 Studio sessions	Duke Ellington	Saja 7 91231-2	1957/ 8	CD	US
*D. E. vol.2 California Dance	Duke Ellington	Saja 7 91042-2	1958	CD	US
*Coltrane and Ellington	John Coltrane	MCAD 39103	9/26/62	CD	US

Name Wormsworth, Jimmy   **Birth Date** 8/14/37

Birthplace Utica, NY   **Reference** Feather (New)

Played with Lambert, Hendricks, and Ross, Phineas Newborn, Al Haig, Hod O'Brien, Allen Eager

Biography NYC. Late '50s - '60s swinging bop drummer—nice brushes—small groups; '70s - '80s Al Haig.

Album Title	Name of Artist	Label w Number	Date Recorded	Format	Country
Jazz Modes	Julius Watkins	Atlantic LP 1280	11/20/58	LP	US
Light foot	Lou Donaldson	Blue Note LP 4053	12/14/58	LP	US
I Love You	Al Haig	Interplay 00281	2/18/77	CD	JA
Renaissance	Allen Eager	Uptown UP 27.09	3/25/82	LP	US

Drummer Discography

Name Wright, Specs   **Birth Date** 9/8/27   2/6/63

Birthplace Philadelphia, PA   **Reference** Grove / Feather (New and '60s)

Played with Julian Adderley, Dizzy Gillespie, Red Garland, Hank Mobley, Lee Morgan, Ray Bryant

Biography NYC. Charles.'50s - early '60s outstanding, not yet well acknowledged. Large, important discography. Swings—fleet, exciting solos— brushes clean, clearly articulated—Red Garland's *Rediscovered Masters vol.2* Prestige OJCCD-769-2.Sometimes confused with "Specs" Powell.

Album Title	Name of Artist	Label w Number	Date Recorded	Format	Country
*Monday Night at Birdland	Hank Mobley	Fresh Sound 031& 032	5/10/55	2 CDs	SP
*Ray Bryant Trio	Ray Bryant	Prestige OJCCD-793-2	4/5/57	CD	US
*Rollins Meets the Big Brass	Sonny Rollins	Verve 815 056-2	7/10/58	CD	US
*Red Garland at the Prelude	Red Garland	Prestige PRCD 24132	10/2/59	CD	US

Name Young, Lee   **Birth Date** 3/7/17

Birthplace New Orleans, LA   **Reference** Grove / Feather (New)

Played with JATP, Lester Young, Nat Cole, Charlie Parker, Benny Goodman

Biography LA. Late '40s - '50s studio and several *Jazz at the Philharmonic* recordings. Brother of Lester— with him, Charlie Parker on JATP dates— included in the 10 CD box *Bird* on Verve 837144-2.

Album Title	Name of Artist	Label w Number	Date Recorded	Format	Country
*Jazz at thePhilharmonic	Norman Granz	Verve MG vol. 1	3/25/46	LP	US
*Jazz at thePhilharmonic	Norman Granz	Verve MG vol. 2	3/25/46	LP	US
Jazz at thePhilharmonic	Norman Granz	Verve MG vol. 3	7/2/44	LP	US
Jazz at thePhilharmonic	Norman Granz	Verve MG vol. 5	7/2/44	LP	US

Name Zelnick, Mel   **Birth Date** 9/28/24

Birthplace New York, NY   **Reference** Feather (New)

Played with Benny Goodman, Wardell Gray, Lennie Tristano, Boyd Raeburn

Biography NYC. Late '40s - '50s swinging bop drummer—recorded with Goodman's small bop bands. Nice brushes. Goodman's *Capitol* recordings have been reissued on *Mosaic* MD-4-148 box set.

Album Title	Name of Artist	Label w Number	Date Recorded	Format	Country
*The Happy Monster	Chubby Jackson	Cool 'N Blue CD 109	5/22/47	CD	SWI
Swedish Pastry	Wardell Gray	Dragon 183	5/27/48	CD	SWE
*Bebop Spoken Here	Benny Goodman	Capitol M-11061	9/9/48	LP/4CD Box	US
Don Eliot (title?)	Don Elliot	Bethlehem BCP 12	2/22/55	LP	US

Name Zitano, Jimmy   **Birth Date** 1/14/28   c. 1992

Birthplace Boston, MA   **Reference** Feather ('60s)

Played with Herb Pomeroy, Charlie Mariano, Serge Chaloff

Biography BOS. '50s Boston —swinging drummer with artists listed. Influenced by Arthur Taylor; early '70s (or late '60s)—to New Orleans with Al Hirt. His discography represents '50s Boston's lively '50's jazz scene.

Album Title	Name of Artist	Label w Number	Date Recorded	Format	Country
High Hat All Stars	Miles Davis	Fresh Sounds 013	1955	CD	SP
*Boston Blow Up	Serge Chaloff	Capitol TOCJ-5374	4/4/55	CD	JA
*Byrd blows on Beacon Hill	Donald Byrd	Transition LP 17	5/7/56	LP	US/JA
Life is many splendored Gig	Herb Pomeroy	Fresh Sounds 084	6/3/57	CD	SP